WE ARE YOUR CHILDREN TOO

Also by P. O'Connell Pearson

Fly Girls
Fighting for the Forest
Conspiracy

WE ARE YOUR CHILDREN TOO

BLACK STUDENTS, WHITE SUPREMACISTS, AND THE BATTLE FOR AMERICA'S SCHOOLS IN PRINCE EDWARD COUNTY, VIRGINIA

P. O'Connell Pearson

Simon & Schuster Books for Young Readers

NEW YORK   LONDON   TORONTO   SYDNEY   NEW DELHI

SIMON & SCHUSTER BOOKS FOR YOUNG READERS
An imprint of Simon & Schuster Children's Publishing Division
1230 Avenue of the Americas, New York, New York 10020
Text © 2023 by Patricia O'Connell Pearson
Jacket illustration © 2023 by Cannaday Chapman
Jacket reference photograph by Hank Walker/The LIFE Picture Collection/Shutterstock
Jacket design by Sarah Creech © 2023 by Simon & Schuster, Inc.
Interior photographs on pages 2, 10, 11, 35, 114, and 145 courtesy of the US National Archives
(photo nos. 76043496, 76043338, 76043502, 532547, 7865621, and 542045); illustrations and
photographs on pages 14, 15, 26, 28, 29, 54, 144, 166, 174, 235, 236, and 237 courtesy of the
Library of Congress Prints and Photographs Division, Washington, DC (photo nos. 2005696251,
2018649129, 2014645928, 99615251, 99615294, 2013646230, 2013649725, 2011648793,
2004672753, 2020720161, 2020720190, 2020720196); photograph on page 24 courtesy of the
Library of Congress, Rare Book and Special Collections Division, Alfred Whital Stern Collection
of Lincolniana (digital ID http://hdl.loc.gov/loc.rbc/lprbscsm.scsm0906); photograph on page
36 courtesy of the National Portrait Gallery, Smithsonian Institution; photographs on pages 39,
141, 142, and 170 courtesy of Virginia Commonwealth University Libraries; photographs on
pages 45 and 220 courtesy of Joan Johns Cobbs and Longwood University; photograph on page
71 courtesy of the Virginia Museum of History and Culture; photograph on page 74 courtesy of
HMdb.org; photograph of illustration on page 75 courtesy of the author, from the book: Simkins,
Francis Butler. *Virginia: History, Government, Geography*. New York: Scribner and Sons, 1957;
photograph on page 92 courtesy of Deloris Hendricks and Longwood University; photograph on
page 96 courtesy of Phyllistine Ward Mosley and Longwood University; photograph on page 103
courtesy of Getty Images; photographs on pages 104 and 214 courtesy of Beverly and John Hines
and Longwood University; photograph on page 124 courtesy of the American Friends Service
Committee Archives; photograph on page 129 courtesy of the John F. Kennedy Presidential
Library and Museum, Boston; photograph on page 148 © Diana Mara Henry; photograph on
page 156 courtesy of Curtis Licensing through Getty; photographs on pages 185, 192, and 193
courtesy of Robert Russa Moton Museum; photograph on page 199 courtesy of James Ghee and
Longwood University; photographs on pages 204 and 212 courtesy of Ken Woodley; photograph
on page 209 by William T. Ziglar, Jr., CC BY-SA 3.0, via Wikimedia Commons; photographs on
pages 218, 221, and 222 courtesy of Christopher Spadone, copyright © Christopher Spadone
SIMON & SCHUSTER BOOKS FOR YOUNG READERS
and related marks are trademarks of Simon & Schuster, Inc.
For information about special discounts for bulk purchases, please contact
Simon & Schuster Special Sales at 1-866-506-1949 or business@simonandschuster.com.
The Simon & Schuster Speakers Bureau can bring authors to your live event.
For more information or to book an event, contact the Simon & Schuster Speakers Bureau at
1-866-248-3049 or visit our website at www.simonspeakers.com.
Interior design by Hilary Zarycky
The text for this book was set in Adobe Caslon Pro.
Manufactured in China
0922 SCP
First Edition
2   4   6   8   10   9   7   5   3   1
CIP data for this book is available from the Library of Congress.
ISBN 9781665901390
ISBN 9781665901413 (ebook)

*For the many men and women of Prince Edward County,
whose resilience and courage inspire*

Contents

WE ARE YOUR CHILDREN TOO

CHAPTER 1

UNEQUAL

FALL 1950

B arbara Johns had been thinking. A lot. That didn't surprise anyone who knew her—her grandmother described the sixteen-year-old as "quiet, serious . . . seemed she had to do a lot of thinking." Her mother said she was "deep."[1] But during the fall of 1950, Barbara was thinking about one thing in particular. One thing that had been bothering her for quite a while. When would something be done about her school—Robert Russa Moton High School in rural Prince Edward County, Virginia?

All the students at Moton High agreed that their school was too small and badly equipped. Parts of it were a damp, drafty, dilapidated disaster. Barbara knew how the other students felt because they frequently talked about it at lunch—a lunch they had to bring from home since the school had no cafeteria. It had no gym, either. Or locker rooms, or science equipment. R. R. Moton High School (named for an educator from the area who had led the Tuskegee Institute in Alabama) had been built at the southern end of the town of Farmville in 1939 and had

Students in an English class at R. R. Moton High School, c. 1951. The stove that heated the "temporary" classroom often sent cinders flying.

space for 180 students. It was sturdy enough—brick with wood floors and tall windows. But by 1950, the student body numbered nearly five hundred, two and a half times the school's capacity. Under pressure from parents and the principal, the county school board had come up with a "temporary" solution: three rickety wooden outbuildings covered in a heavy paper coated with tar—the thick, black liquid used in roadbuilding. Often seen on chicken coops, the tar paper was supposed to keep rain out, but it didn't do its job very well at all. And it seemed that when members of the school board said "temporary," they actually meant "permanent."

Not only did the "tar paper shacks"—as everyone called them—leak, but their only heat came from woodburning potbellied stoves at one end of each long, low structure. In winter, students sitting near the stoves felt ready to combust, while students in the back of the room wore their heavy coats during class. Hot coals sometimes jumped out of the stoves onto the wood floor, forcing whoever was nearby to scoop them back into the stove before the building caught fire.[2] Students from other schools laughed and said the shacks looked like chicken coops. It was embarrassing. Worse, the shacks didn't come close to solving the overcrowding problem.

Several teachers had to meet their classes in the main building's auditorium—really just a big room with folding chairs and a small stage—where the noise of many classes going on at once was terrible. Plus, the building was designed so that students moving from one wing of the school to the other had to walk through that auditorium, adding to the distractions. Some teachers taught classes in old, abandoned school buses parked beside the building. Others met their students outside unless it was raining.

Barbara and the other students complained about more than the actual buildings. There weren't enough books to go around in most classes, and the books the school did have were old, out-of-date, and worn. Classroom equipment—

desks, chairs, blackboards, and the rest—was old and worn too. And there were never enough basic supplies like paper or chalk.

Even getting to school was a challenge. Students came late or missed whole days because the secondhand school buses the county provided broke down frequently. Other children had to walk miles from the farms where they lived because the county didn't provide a school bus for them at all. John Stokes and his twin sister, Carrie, were eager to learn. Eager enough to walk four and a half miles along the gravel shoulder of a very busy highway to get to the overcrowded, poorly supplied Moton High School every day, no matter what the weather was like. Four and a half miles—at least an hour and a half of walking each way—to get to classes in leaky, temporary buildings. John Stokes commented that the cows he milked had nicer buildings than the students at Moton did.[3]

Imagine the determination it took for a young person to face that kind of discomfort, difficulty, even danger, every day just to go to school. For some students who didn't plan to go to college or trade school, a high school diploma didn't seem worth the terrible effort. Many were tempted to drop out, and who could blame them? Barbara Johns, who wanted very much to go to college, never considered quitting. But the idea of two more years at Moton was depressing, especially when after-school activities took her to other counties and she saw what their schools were like.

Barbara was a good student and a generally cheerful, rather quiet, person. But as much as she liked and respected her teachers and the principal, and as much as she enjoyed learning, R. R. Moton High School was wearing her down. It was wearing everyone down.

At sixteen, Barbara looked younger than her age. She had wide-set, almond-shaped brown eyes; dark, shoulder-length hair; and a big smile that lit up her whole face. She was soft-spoken, but not afraid to say what she thought, and she was comfortable talking to adults, the school music teacher in particular. Miss Inez Davenport made Barbara feel like she could tell the teacher almost anything. One day, when the situation at Moton High School had really gotten to her, Barbara told Miss Davenport just how fed up she was. It wasn't fair, she said, that she and all the other students had to attend a school with such dreadful equipment and miserable facilities.

Barbara felt bolder as she talked to Miss Davenport that day, and finally said that she was "sick and tired" of being stuck with such a school. Miss Davenport thought for a minute and then said, "Why don't you do something about it?"[4]

Was her favorite teacher dismissing her? Barbara wondered. Didn't Miss Davenport care? Hurt and unable to think of anything to say, Barbara turned and left the room. But she couldn't push Miss Davenport's words out of her head. Was it possible that the woman wasn't being sarcastic? Could she have meant it? Maybe there *was* something Barbara could do. But what?

Barbara thought long and hard about what action she could take, but no ideas came to her. Parents had argued with the school board year after year, pleading for better facilities for their children. Principal M. Boyd Jones had repeatedly asked the school superintendent to do something. The school board made promises and more promises, but nothing ever happened. If parents and the school principal couldn't get the school board to make improvements, how could a sixteen-year-old?

The Johnses' family farm lay in the soft hills southwest of Farmville, where dark green pine forests stood out against the yellower green of tobacco fields and pastures. Each spring brought a thousand more shades of green. Barbara liked to spend quiet time in her favorite shady spot in the woods when she could get away from her younger siblings. There she could let go of her frustration and imagine miracles. She wrote later about her dreams that a wonderful rich person had swooped in to fix everything at school. Or that a huge storm had destroyed the school, and then out of the wreck "rose a magnificent building and all the students were joyous. . . ." But she knew no miracle was likely. While she fed the pigs or collected eggs or did any of her many chores, she brooded about how awful her school was. What made the situation especially painful was that just down the road from R. R. Moton High School stood Farmville High School, a well-built, well-equipped, well-supplied, spacious public school—a school she and John Stokes and the others weren't allowed to attend.[5]

The days went by, and still Barbara had no idea what she or anyone else could do to convince the Prince Edward County School Board to repair or replace the school. She was busy with homework and with the drama club, the chorus, and the student council. Whenever she had any free time, she read. And read. Every kind of book she could find. She wasn't allowed to go to the public library in town, but her uncle Vernon Johns, who lived in Alabama, kept shelves and shelves of books in her grandmother's house. He encouraged Barbara and the other children to make use of those books. They took her to places where roofs didn't leak and schoolbooks weren't worn. They helped fuel her dreams. But finding time to read was hard.

Violet Johns, Barbara's mother, worked for the US Navy in Washington, DC, nearly two hundred miles from home. The family needed the money she earned there, so

Mrs. Johns stayed in DC during the week and came back to Prince Edward County on weekends. With Barbara's father, Robert, working the farm, it was up to Barbara to care for her younger sister, Joan, and their three brothers. She fixed their breakfasts, packed their lunches, made sure they were clean and dressed, and got them onto the school bus every morning. She cooked dinner every night.

One morning, Barbara struggled to get the children out the door and down the hill to meet the bus on time. Only when they got to the stop did she realize that she'd left her own lunch in the house. She ran up the hill and grabbed it but couldn't get back before the bus came, and her siblings couldn't get the driver to wait. Barbara, a student who never missed class and never "ditched" school, had no way to get there. It was much too far to walk—some fifteen miles. She waited, hoping a neighbor on the way to Farmville might come by and give her a lift. Then she saw a big yellow school bus coming. She knew where it was going, and she knew what was about to happen.

The half-empty bus was on its way right past Moton High School to Farmville High School—the one with the cafeteria and gym and science labs and enough books and heat and . . . The bus went by. The driver would not stop for Barbara, though it was obvious where she was headed. She wasn't a bit surprised.

Barbara Johns had always known why her school's facilities were overcrowded and pathetic and the other school's facilities were very good. She knew why the school board would do nothing to improve Moton High School. And she knew on this morning why she couldn't get a ride to school on a half-empty bus. The students on that bus were White, and she was Black. They attended the White high school, and she attended the Black high school. In Prince Edward County's White-run school system, their education mattered. Hers didn't.

The inequality that hit Barbara Johns so forcefully that day in late 1950 wasn't new. The differences between Prince Edward County's Moton High School and its Farmville High School weren't new either. And they weren't unusual in the United States. All over the South, states and counties required separate schools for White and Black children—schools with the same kinds of differences Barbara saw in Moton High and Farmville High. Generally, White children went every day to tidy buildings that were far better kept and better supplied than Black schools were. Northern states didn't have laws separating White and Black students, yet those students often ended up in very different circumstances anyway. It had gone on for generations. But on this morning, as Barbara Johns watched the White students' bus pass her by, she knew it was time for change.

The auditorium at Farmville High School, c. 1951.

Later she wrote,

> Right then and there, I decided something had
> to be done about this inequality. . . . All day
> my mind and thoughts were whirling and as
> I lay in my bed that night—I prayed for help.
> That night . . . a plan began to formulate in my
> mind.[6]

Barbara knew that any demand for a better school
building was risky—especially in a place like Prince
Edward County. She worried about how the county's
White leaders would react to such a demand. Still, she had

The auditorium at R. R. Moton High School, c. 1951.

to try. She had to try for herself and for her younger sister and brothers. But as she considered her plan, Barbara Johns had no idea that she was about to make history. No idea that her plan would lead to years of struggle for something much bigger than she imagined. She may not have thought about it, but Barbara Johns was going up against more than three hundred years of Virginia history, of American history.

Inequality and injustice in Prince Edward County had started long before public schools existed and more than one hundred fifty years before there was a United States Constitution. That's a lot of history. But the story of Prince Edward County's schools in the twentieth century doesn't make sense without starting at the beginning. History is like that. One event connects to another and then another. Those connections help to explain the past and much of the present. Many parts of United States history make Americans proud. But sadly, inequality is also a part of the history of the United States. It's an ugly and difficult part of history. But it's a part of history every American needs to know.

CHAPTER 2

HARD HISTORY

1607–1950

Virginia was Great Britain's first colony on the East Coast of North America. A group of British men landed there in 1607 and made Jamestown the colony's first permanent settlement. The men were amazed by the area's rich wildlife and lush vegetation. They'd never seen anything like it. People of the local tribes, part of the Powhatan Confederacy, lived there comfortably—hunting, fishing, and farming as their ancestors had for centuries. They helped the settlers at first, but turned against them when the newcomers kept demanding food instead of learning to grow it themselves and took Powhatan hunting lands. Many colonists soon died from disease and hunger. Others died in conflicts with the native people. But the Jamestown settlement survived and eventually succeeded with tobacco as its major product. How does that connect to Barbara Johns in the middle of the twentieth century? Well . . .

Twelve years after the first colonists arrived, in 1619, an English ship carrying kidnapped Africans from Angola landed in Virginia. The English had taken the captive African men and women from a Portuguese slave ship and sold or traded these people for supplies when they reached Virginia. "Sold." That's a terrible word to apply to human beings, but that's what happened.

A 1901 illustration of Africans from a Dutch ship landing at Jamestown in 1619.

A count of Virginia's population in 1625 listed 1,232 people. Several thousand colonists had died in the eighteen years since the founding of Jamestown, and officials did not include native people in their count. The population included twenty-two servants—all either Africans or of African descent. The word "slave" wasn't used in census counts until later, and records show that some African servants gained freedom and made their own lives in the colony. Most did not. They were enslaved for life. In 1661, race-based slavery became legal. It would remain legal for the next 204 years.[7]

By 1700, the owners of huge farms called *plantations*

Field-workers cultivate tobacco, 1904.

in Virginia and several other Southern colonies relied on enslaved people to do the enormous work of growing and harvesting their crops. The enslaved population grew rapidly through births and more arrivals from Africa, where African slavers kidnapped men, women, and children and sold them to European traders.

Did the colonists think this was acceptable? Moral? Tragically, most colonists probably did. Many may not have thought about the right or wrong of it at all. Various types of forced labor had existed throughout history, often the result of victors enslaving prisoners of war. People were used to the idea of it.

By the late 1600s, though, a different kind of slavery developed in the Americas. While earlier enslaved people could usually buy or earn freedom, most enslaved people in North and South America could not. They lived in bondage for their entire lives. And though the children of those earlier enslaved people were not born into slavery, slavery passed from one generation to the next in the Americas.

There was another key difference as well. The colonists shared a belief that was common in England and other European countries at the time. They thought that their culture and people were superior to other cultures and people in all sorts of ways. Throughout history, groups of people in many parts of the world have believed in their own superiority over other groups. Europeans' ideas of superiority included the belief that God wanted them to rule "inferior people" and convert those people to Christianity. And Europeans argued that they had every right to conquer and colonize non-Christian populations as they "discovered" them. By the 1600s, Europeans began to tie their ideas of superiority to skin color as well.

These ideas and beliefs allowed European settlers to take land and hunting and fishing grounds from native peoples without feeling guilt. Their beliefs allowed them to enslave African captives and their descendants as well. And the European settlers passed their beliefs on to their children and grandchildren. Today we refer to the beliefs and attitudes that allow White people to keep power for themselves and deny it to everyone else as *White supremacy*.

In 1776, a century and a half after settling Jamestown, thirteen British colonies broke away from Great Britain to form the United States. The new nation adopted the US Constitution in 1788, and George Washington became the country's first president in April, 1789. At the time, slavery legally existed in every state except Massachusetts. But the 1790 census showed that over 90 percent of enslaved people lived in the South.

Virginia had the biggest state population overall at that time, and the biggest enslaved population. Enslaved people made up some 40 percent of all recorded Virginians (Indigenous or native people were, once again, not counted in the census). Most enslaved people worked on plantations.

Prince Edward County's gentle hills and rich soil produced wheat, corn, hay, apples, peaches, and more. But there, and throughout south central Virginia in the early 1800s, tobacco was the biggest and most profitable crop and had been for 150 years. While tobacco brought many planters wealth, however, it required more workers than any other crop. By the time of the 1850 census, enslaved Black men, women, and children made up 60 percent of Prince Edward County's population. Some of those people were Barbara Johns's ancestors.

Old census records are often difficult to interpret, and historians cannot be sure how many people in the South held enslaved workers. But many scholars agree that probably less than one-third of all Southern White families were enslavers. (A small number of Black and Native American families also held enslaved workers.) Most White enslavers had small farms and held a small number of enslaved people.

About ten percent of White slave-holding families owned plantations and controlled more than twenty enslaved workers. These plantation owners were known as "planters." Planters, primarily the men who headed plantation families, controlled half of the more four million enslaved people in the South.

Think about that. Think about the small number of Southern White men—perhaps some 45,000 or so—who controlled the lives of two million Black men, women, and children in bondage. Think of the enormous wealth and power those men had. Not only did they control their own lands, the people they enslaved, and the money that the land and the people represented, but they also controlled the South's economy and its politics.

Many planters thought that they were good "masters" and took good care of "their people." They claimed they were not cruel, and it made financial sense to "care for" enslaved people because those people were worth a lot of money. But those planters were enslavers. And even under enslavers who didn't beat or starve enslaved people for no reason, the threats of hunger and violence hung in the air that every enslaved person breathed. White enslavers had the right to beat, whip, rape, sell, and even kill enslaved Black people. White men and women who held enslaved workers defended the system of slavery. So did many White people who were not slaveholders. At first, they said that slavery was necessary for a successful economy. As time went on, they used the Bible to justify slavery. They also argued that Black people couldn't take care of themselves, couldn't govern themselves or earn a living on their own. Black people needed White people, they said.

Yet powerful White planters feared that Black men and women would organize and rebel. So they kept their Black workers from earning more than a tiny amount of money on their own and kept them from meeting in large groups or hearing news from other parts of the country. Every morning and evening they counted axes and shovels and anything else someone might use as a weapon. White legislators even passed laws against teaching an enslaved person to read or write. Why? Because education is power. And whatever White enslavers argued about slavery being good for the enslaved, or about Black people being inferior to White, the evidence against those arguments was clear. Black men and women proved themselves every day—especially in Prince Edward County.

Free Black people had formed the community of Israel Hill in Prince Edward County soon after 1800. They built their lives and homes on a tract of land they inherited from the man who had once held them as slaves. During most of the eighteenth century, Virginia law had made it very difficult to free enslaved people. But the ideals of the American Revolution had nudged a lot of White people to think about the morality of slavery, and Virginia legislators had changed the law in 1782. Some Virginia slaveholders then freed the people they had enslaved, often in their wills. Several thousand Black Virginians gained freedom this way. But most slaveholders did not free anyone.

Richard Randolph, a cousin of Thomas Jefferson, saw the evil of slavery. When he wrote his will at the age of twenty-five, he condemned slavery and the legal circumstances that kept him from immediately freeing the enslaved people his father had left to him (though, there were two or three people he could have freed but didn't). Randolph died the next year in 1796. Arguments over the will delayed his wishes for several years, but by 1810, some ninety freed people began building Israel Hill.

Over the next six decades, the men and women of the Israel Hill community, as well as their children and grandchildren, farmed, bought, and sold land and buildings in the county and in Farmville, and opened small businesses. Some worked for White neighbors at the same pay that

White workers got. Free Black men couldn't vote or serve on juries at the time, but they could *file*, or submit, lawsuits in court and sometimes did, even against White people. The men and women of the Israel Hill community, and free Black people in other parts of the South, proved that arguments in defense of slavery were lies. They proved that Black men and women were just as capable as anyone else.

The United States grew in size and population, and Northern and Southern states moved in different directions. In the North, towns and cities sprang up and industry developed. Slavery decreased as factory owners turned to European immigrants to fill the need for labor. They paid these men, women, and children extremely low wages to work in terrible conditions, but many immigrants, especially children, found opportunities to make better lives. In the South, some planters continued to grow tobacco, rice, or indigo, while others turned to cotton as their major crop. All required huge numbers of workers, and slavery increased.

By the middle of the 1800s, most Northern states had outlawed slavery, and the differences between the North and the South became serious conflicts. There was plenty to argue about—taxes for canals and railroads, tariffs (a kind of tax) on European goods, what to do with newly acquired lands in the West, how much power the federal government should have. But one issue stood out above all the others: slavery. Slavery mattered in a way that nothing else did. While all the other arguments could be worked out through compromise, slavery could not—though Congress tried in 1820 and 1850 and 1854 to make an agreement that would last. By the late 1850s, slavery was *the* issue—the issue of real importance.

Most Northerners disliked the idea of slavery. But they weren't *abolitionists*—they weren't ready to force an end to slavery in the Southern states. However, they did support banning slavery in territories and new states in the West. That would mean more free states (states that banned slavery) than states that protected slavery, and therefore more members of Congress from free states. White Southerners objected. They knew that if new states banned slavery, White Southerners would lose their power in Congress to pass federal laws protecting slavery.

Presidential candidate Abraham Lincoln agreed that the nation should ban slavery in the West. But he said that he would not try to end slavery in the South. Even so, White Southerners saw him as a threat to their way of life and their economy—all based on slavery. When he won the presidential election in 1860, powerful White people in Southern states refused to accept the election results. South Carolina voted to *secede*. Within months, ten other states, including Virginia, also voted to secede—leave the

United States and join together to establish their own country. They called the country the Confederate States of America, and they wrote a constitution that protected slavery, saying, "No . . . law denying or impairing the right of property in negro slaves shall be passed." Lincoln rejected the possibility of secession. These states were not a new nation, he said. These were states in rebellion. He was determined to save the Union of all the states—the United States of America.

In the end, the tragedy of slavery led to the tragedy of the American Civil War.

Not every Confederate soldier fought to keep people enslaved. Not every soldier in the United States army fought to end slavery. But slavery caused the civil war, and the civil war killed more Americans, military and civilian, than any other war in United States history. Between 1861 and 1865, some 750,000 people—2.5 percent of the total population—died of disease or of wounds suffered in horrific battles (2.5 percent of today's population is over 8,000,000). More United States Army soldiers died fighting the Confederacy than died fighting any foreign war before or since. The rebellious states lost the war, and the Confederacy ceased to exist. So did slavery as Lincoln and most Northerners came to support *emancipation*—freeing all enslaved people.

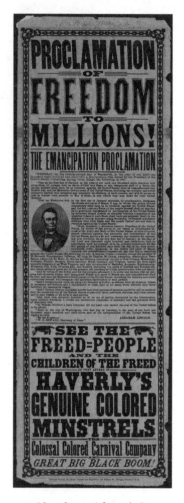

Abraham Lincoln's Emancipation Proclamation as printed by the National Printing Company in Chicago. The document is bordered by chains.

During the war, Lincoln issued the 1863 Emancipation Proclamation, officially ending slavery in the rebelling states. Those states, of course, didn't view Lincoln as their president and ignored the proclamation. The document didn't apply to the four slave states that had not rebelled or seceded—Maryland, Delaware, Kentucky, and Missouri. But the Emancipation Proclamation held enormous symbolism. Despite White slaveholders' attempts to keep Black workers from hearing outside news, enslaved people knew about the proclamation. As long as the United States survived and the Confederacy died, their children would never be sold away again. As the war went on, thousands of

Black Americans—individuals, whole families, men and women—escaped from their captors and found their way to US Army camps and freedom. And some 180,000 Black men enlisted in the US Army to join the fight.[8]

Soon after the war ended in 1865, the Thirteenth Amendment became part of the US Constitution. It banned slavery forever. By then, much of the South—where almost all of the war's battles had occurred—lay in ruins. Two thirds of those battles had been fought in Virginia.

Amending the Constitution

The framers of the US Constitution knew that their plan for government would need to change over time as the country changed. So they spelled out in Article V a process for making changes through amendments. The process is difficult because the framers did not want people to change the Constitution without careful thought. Nearly 12,000 amendments have been proposed since 1789. Only twenty-seven have been ratified or approved. There are two ways to approve amendments, but only one of them has been used during the last 235 years. Congress approves the amendment by a two-thirds majority vote in both the Senate and House of Representatives, and then at least three fourths of state legislatures ratify it.

Richmond, Virginia, capital of the Confederacy, in ruins, 1865.

Prince Edward County almost escaped the destruction that so much of Virginia experienced. But the desperate battles fought there in the last few weeks of the war left the county in tatters. Unusable roads and bridges; trampled farmland that couldn't support crops; ruined barns; cattle, sheep, hogs, and horses taken or killed. Farms in Prince Edward didn't produce as much as they had before the war until 1940, seventy-five years later.

Confederate money was now useless, banks had nothing

to lend, and there was no postal service. Most people in the county—Black and White—had to stand in line to get food handouts from federal troops. Without those handouts they could very well have starved, but the humiliation was terrible. Across the South, the war had turned everything upside down. Enslaved people were now free but had no homes, jobs, money, or education. Plantation owners were as needy as poor folk. And the clear-cut rules for relationships between planters and enslaved workers, between White people and Black people, were gone. No one knew what would come next.[9]

Think of the questions that newly freed people faced. Where would they go? Where would they live? How would they earn a living? Would they be able to find family members who'd been sold away to other slaveholders or who'd run away to freedom? Freedom was an answer to two hundred years of prayer, and no one wanted to go back. But going forward wasn't going to be easy.

White Southerners faced an uncertain future too. Many small towns and counties had lost nearly all their young men. That left thousands of widows with no money, and thousands of farms and businesses with no one to work them. A lot of land was ruined, and planters whose land could still grow crops had no money to pay workers. Most White families felt heartbreak for the men they had lost, of course. But they also felt fear for the future and anger at the destruction they saw everywhere. They blamed Northerners and the United States government for the war and despised the federal troops who stayed in the South for the next five years.

Clara Brim, formerly enslaved as a child, in
Beaumont, Texas, 1937.

Andrew Goodman, formerly enslaved as a child, in Dallas, Texas, 1937.

Some Southern White men and women went west or even to other countries after the war. Others tried to adjust and move forward. A few felt relief that slavery was over. But most stayed where they were and held on to their old beliefs. While the Confederacy had died, White supremacist beliefs remained strong.

Some formerly enslaved individuals and families also went west for a fresh start and a chance to own land or herd cattle. But most stayed on the same land they'd lived on before. Since landowners had no cash, a new system developed. Recently freed Black people, and some poor White people, worked the land and then shared the profits from the harvested crops with the landowner (the landowner got most of the profit) in a system called *sharecropping*. Others rented land from a landowner and farmed it. Some found paying jobs as cooks, maids, stable hands, and the like. Eventually some Black families managed to buy their own farmland. Even with hard work, though, the vast majority of Black men and women stayed poor.

In the meantime, the US Congress passed laws that would make real progress possible. The government opened schools for formerly enslaved and free Black children and adults. Black communities started their own schools as well. They had freedom now, and that included the freedom to learn. They wasted no time. Young students crowded into tiny buildings or gathered outside to learn. Many adults took classes at night. That was hard after a long day working in the fields. But it was worth it to be educated.

Amendments to the Constitution opened doors too. The Fourteenth Amendment said that the law must apply equally to everyone—laws could not be different for Black Americans and White Americans. The Fifteenth Amendment guaranteed that states could not keep people from voting based on their race, though no women of any color could vote yet. Black men now registered to vote and served on juries. They could run for office. Tazewell Branch, for example, had been born into slavery in Prince Edward County and was in his late thirties when the end of the Civil War brought freedom. He learned to read and write, became a shoemaker, bought land, and served on Farmville's town council. In 1873, Branch was elected to Virginia's legislature and won reelection two years later.

• • •

During those same years, most Americans in the North and West put the war behind them. The Transcontinental Railroad, built by thousands of Chinese and Irish immigrant laborers, connected the East and West Coasts for the first time. Populations and businesses grew in the North and across the Midwest and West, and new opportunities attracted millions more immigrants.

In the South, only a few White men moved on. Instead, most worked to regain the power they'd had before the Civil War. Those men were afraid. They were frightened of being a minority in areas where the majority of citizens were Black. They were frightened of losing status and power, frightened of change. Some formed terrorist groups like the Ku Klux Klan (KKK) to intimidate Black people and "keep them in their place"—even if that meant murder. Others pushed state governments to ignore or work around the new amendments and federal laws that protected Black citizens' rights.

Black men and women saw their progress torn away, especially after the Supreme Court ruled in 1896 that being *separate* did not mean being *unequal,* and that segregation based on race did not violate the Constitution. This idea of "separate but equal" soon spilled into every corner of life in the South as White supremacists pushed for complete segregation.

The secessionist states had had to write new state constitutions as they'd reentered the Union of the United States. Virginia's 1868 constitution guaranteed Black men the right to vote and established public schools in the state for the first time. Many Virginians thought the future looked promising. Thirty-four years later, however, a small group of a hundred or so White men decided to give Virginia a future that looked just like the past. They pushed through a new state constitution.

The 1902 constitution required Virginia voters to pass a "literacy" test proving they understood the state constitution. Black citizens usually had to answer much more difficult questions than White citizens did—often nearly impossible questions. Voters also had to pay a *poll tax*—a fee for voting. Those measures didn't directly violate the Fifteenth Amendment, but they worked to keep almost all Black men and many poor White men from voting. That meant that citizens like Tazewell Branch wouldn't be elected to office any longer. One state senator said, "Discrimination . . . is precisely what we propose . . . to the elimination of every negro voter who can be gotten rid of."[10]

The new constitution also made segregation in public places and in businesses legal, and it required that public schools be segregated. The 1902 constitution pushed racism and segregation into Virginia's legal system, education system, and economic system. It made *systemic racism*—racism built into people's lives—part of Virginia's highest law. The all-White state legislature soon passed new laws known as *Jim Crow*—a term used to insult Black men and based on a slow, clumsy character in old theater productions. Those laws required segregation at banks, restaurants, hotels, schools, parks, libraries, and just about everywhere else.

At the same time, White organizations such as the United Daughters of the Confederacy raised money for monuments and statues glorifying the old Confederacy and its leaders. Silently but publicly those monuments told White people that their ancestors had fought and died for a noble cause. That cause wasn't made clear, but Southern White children learned that the cause was *not* slavery. Their ancestors had died for their families and homes and way of life (a White way of life that depended on slavery).

The same monuments reminded Black people of the horror that they or their ancestors had suffered.

White political leaders and Confederate Daughters made the Confederate monuments centerpieces in small towns and big cities. They organized Fourth of July celebrations in front of the monuments even though the Confederacy had officially rejected the words of the Declaration of Independence—"All men are created equal." White families picnicked in front of the memorials.

White children stood at the bases of the statues for class pictures. Step by step, this group of White Southerners rewrote history—intentionally. And everyone, White and Black, understood that the Confederate statues, memorials, and monuments they saw every day were symbols of a new kind of White power.

Black leaders fought back against Jim Crow and the terror of the KKK. In 1909, they formed the National Association for the Advancement of Colored People (NAACP) to defend Black Americans and use the legal system to make change. Individuals looked for change too, and found new opportunities when World War I began in Europe in 1914.

The United States suddenly needed all sorts of military equipment and other war goods. Busy factories needed workers. Thousands of poor Black tenant farmers and sharecroppers streamed from the rural South to Northern cities to fill those jobs. They didn't find equality—there was ugly racism in the North as well as the South—but they did find better pay, sometimes equal pay, and open doors at businesses and schools. This *Great Migration* continued without slowing for the next fifteen years.

The war also brought thousands of Black men into the military. They served in segregated units and proved themselves again and again. Imagine their disappointment when they came home and saw that attitudes hadn't

Six Black soldiers who almost died trying to rescue a drowning marine in the surf at Iwo Jima. From left to right, back row: Technician L. C. Carter, Jr., Private John Bonner, Jr.; Staff Sergeant Charles R. Johnson. Front row, from left to right: Technician A. B. Randle, Technician Homer H. Gaines, and Private Willie Tellie. March 11, 1945.

changed. But their experiences gave them new skills, confidence, and pride.

The same thing happened in an even larger way during World War II (1939–1945). A second wave of the Great Migration changed the nation's population. And more than a million Black soldiers and sailors, including Barbara Johns's father and John Stokes's older brothers, served bravely in the still-segregated military. Those men returned after the war hoping that their service and

Jackie Robinson was the first Black player in Major League Baseball in the twentieth century. He led the Brooklyn Dodgers to six pennants and a World Series championship.

patriotism had changed feelings at home. But they found little difference in attitudes after the war. They didn't even receive the same government benefits as White soldiers. Despite it all, the men had good reason to be proud and to stand tall, confident that they had served their country well. Many were ready to demand their rights.

In the years just after the Second World War, the push for racial equality grew stronger with the NAACP leading the way and working to make civil rights a national issue. The Brooklyn Dodgers made history when Black first baseman Jackie Robinson started playing for the team in 1947. Baseball did not fall apart and Robinson was named Rookie of the Year. The following year, President Harry Truman ordered an end to segregation in the US armed forces. The military didn't fall apart, either.

It seemed the country really could make progress even while many White Americans held on to their prejudices. That progress, though, was slow and difficult. Prince Edward County, Virginia, would prove just how slow and difficult any progress could be.

CHAPTER 3

STRIKE

1951

B arbara Johns and the other students at R. R. Moton High School in 1950 had grown up with segregation. Their parents tried to protect them from the sting of prejudice, but the children couldn't avoid seeing Jim Crow discrimination in Farmville. The town was home to just 5,000 people and had only six or seven blocks in its business district. Most of the brick buildings along those streets were no more than two stories high. But Farmville was the biggest town for many miles around. Aside from small general stores in the countryside, it was the only place to buy food or clothes or anything else without driving an hour or more. The parents of many Moton students worked in Farmville, some at their own businesses, many others in White people's houses or in the tall brick tobacco warehouses that stood along the bank of the Appomattox River at the north end of town.

Black and White people in Farmville lived near each other and often worked next to one another. Black women cleaned White families' homes, washed their clothes,

Main Street in Farmville, Virginia, 1963.

cooked their food, and took care of their children. But Black residents, older and younger, understood that while it was all right to go into a restaurant to order food, they couldn't sit in the restaurant to eat what they ordered. They could buy things at most stores but could not try on clothing or shoes or return anything that didn't fit. They could not handle merchandise. The bowling alley and the State Theater were off-limits. So were parks and the public library. The hospital had a few beds set aside for Black people, but Black doctors couldn't go into the hospital to see or treat their patients.

Most Black families worked within and around the rules as best they could. Many bought their clothes and shoes from catalogs. They made their own food or went to Black-owned places. They created their own entertainment and social life, frequently centered on their churches.

When Black people of any age stepped out of their homes or community, they were careful, always alert for possible trouble. That was something Black children learned very early. As John Stokes described it, "I walked on eggs, and I stayed out of harm's way."[11] It was more complicated than knowing where to go and where not to go. It was more complicated than knowing how to act in each White-owned business.

Black children in Prince Edward County and many other places around the country had to know how to keep themselves safe from White violence by the time they started school. The lessons grew more important for older children and teens (Black children today learn very similar lessons).

John Stokes recalled being out after dark one evening when he was twelve. He was walking the four miles to his home from Farmville after a Boy Scout meeting when he heard a car coming. He knew the rules. He'd dressed in dark clothes as his parents had taught him and now raced for cover in a thicket of big bushes as the car slowed to a stop. He'd done the same thing before. But on this hot, sticky, very dark night, John ran into a barbed-wire fence, tearing his clothes and his skin. He didn't dare cry out at the pain or try to stop the slimy wet blood running down his leg. He stayed as still as a fence post, hardly breathing while his heart pounded in his chest, until the White men who had stepped out of the car got back in and drove off.[12]

Imagine knowing at ten or twelve that a passing car might carry White men or teenagers ready to hurt or even kill a child for no reason. Imagine knowing that the police—all of them White men and often White supremacists—weren't likely to be of any help and might make things worse with fake accusations. Violence didn't occur as often in Prince Edward County as it did in some other parts of the South, but Black children couldn't take chances. They reminded themselves every day to stay alert, to keep their eyes and ears open for danger—always.

There were more rules. A young Black man must never, ever, ever talk to a White woman or be alone with her. Ever. Black people of any age mustn't argue with or contradict a White person no matter what. Black and White children could play together and even go into each other's homes to eat when they were quite young. But as they got older, they couldn't play with each other anymore. In Prince Edward, the children's backyards might meet, their parents' businesses might be side by side on the same street, their family farms might adjoin, but after a certain age Black and White children were no longer free to play together. Why?

Most White people didn't say it out loud, but they feared that if Black and White youngsters played happily together and liked each other as small children, they might continue to like each other as older children. That could lead to dating, which could lead to marriage (though marriages between people of different races were illegal at the time) and children with one Black parent and one White parent. White supremacists found that idea terrifying. They believed they had to protect the "purity" of the White race at all costs. As if such a thing had ever existed in the first place.

Naturally, Black Americans despised having every piece of their lives dictated to them. They wanted change, but many older men and women were afraid to make demands in 1950, and with good reason. Landlords could evict people who rented their homes or farmland. White employers could fire anyone who acted "uppity." Black parents worried that if they made demands, they would lose their jobs and be unable to feed their children. And what were the chances of accomplishing anything in a place where most White people approved of segregation and discrimination? Black citizens couldn't win in court with all-White judges and juries. They couldn't win with an all-White police force, or with the all-White school board or all-White county board of supervisors (the group of men elected to run the county). And they couldn't vote for change since White laws and intimidation kept them from registering to vote.

The fact is that no matter what Prince Edward County and other places like it called themselves, they were not democracies. They were not representative governments. When half of adult citizens cannot elect representatives or serve on juries and school boards, a republic or representative democracy does not exist. Many Black citizens of Prince Edward County put up with the system because they couldn't afford to move away or didn't want to sell family-owned land or leave friends and extended family. They put up with it on the surface, though not in their hearts and minds. And they pushed for change where they could, especially when it came to the county's Black schools.

Representative Government

"Democracy" means "rule by the people," from the Greek word for people—"démos." In a democracy the people rule either directly by making decisions on laws and policies, or indirectly by electing representatives to make and carry out laws for them. A representative democracy such as the United States is also called a republic.

By 1950, though, more Black people, especially young people, had begun to believe that equality and actual democracy might be possible. If that were true, it was worth taking risks. Barbara Johns thought that way. Her parents and grandparents were proud people. They had the advantage of owning their land—they couldn't be evicted. And Barbara had grown up listening to her uncle Vernon whenever he visited from Alabama.

The Reverend Vernon Johns liked to recite long poems and whole books of the Bible from memory. He could read Latin, Greek, and Hebrew. He'd traveled all over the country giving powerful speeches and sermons that challenged listeners to act. In 1950, Reverend Johns was the pastor of the Dexter Avenue Baptist Church in Montgomery, Alabama. Martin Luther King, Jr., would pastor there a few years later.[13]

Johns was known for his dreadful temper and had a reputation as a *firebrand*—someone who stirs up trouble. Barbara had a temper herself, something her sister and brothers knew. But she had no interest in causing trouble, even though she feared that her plans to get a better school might do just that. In all her dreaming, she never considered making demands of stores or theaters or bowling alleys or anything else. She didn't expect to overthrow the school board or the board of supervisors. And she wanted to protect her teachers and principal. Barbara wasn't asking for anything as risky as desegregation. She simply wanted a school that wasn't overcrowded, leaky, and smelly. That didn't seem too much to ask.

Once she formulated the idea for getting a better school, Barbara worked alone on the details. She wanted the student body at R. R. Moton High School to go on

Barbara Johns in her graduation photo in 1952.

strike—refuse to go to school until the school board did something. Later she said that her father "would have considered it foolish." She admitted, though, that "he wouldn't have stopped me. . . . As he put it I was too stubborn . . . anyway."[14] Barbara's mother was working in Washington during the week, and when they saw each other on the weekends, Barbara didn't say anything to her, either. She didn't even think of talking to Uncle Vernon about it. And she didn't mention it to her friends or sister and brothers. They might not have been able to keep a secret, and the plan had to remain secret if it was going to work. But she needed help, so she developed a second plan for getting the right people to work with her.

As Barbara described it,

> That plan was to assemble together the student council members whom I considered the "creme de la cream" [the best] of the school—because they were smart and thinkers. I knew them and trusted them and I was a part of them. From this we would formulate plans to go on a strike.[15]

The first students she contacted were twins John and Carrie Stokes. Like the Johns family, the Stokes family owned their own farm, and Mr. and Mrs. Stokes were well known in the county, respected by White residents as well as Black residents. John and Carrie had the respect of their fellow students, too—he was president of the senior class and she was vice president. Besides that, Barbara knew that John and Carrie had traveled outside the South. Their older sister, an army nurse stationed in New Jersey, had taken them on a trip to New York City. John wrote that he could hardly believe what he'd experienced. He rode in the front of a crowded bus and no one objected. He saw Black men and women working in good jobs. He sat next to White fans at Ebbets Field to watch Jackie Robinson play baseball with the Brooklyn Dodgers. And when they went to his sister's army post, he saw "people working and living together for the good of a cause, and the sky was not falling on any of them."[16]

The Stokes twins were the kind of partners Barbara needed. They agreed to meet on the bleachers outside, where no one would hear their conversation. They continued meeting into the winter, keeping everything secret. Slowly and carefully, they recruited other students who were "smart and thinkers" as Barbara had said. Students who could keep quiet and who came from various parts of the county. Like Barbara and the Stokeses, most of them had seen bits of the world outside Prince Edward County and knew the possibilities. And they saw their own situation clearly.

Some of the group's members had attended elementary schools with no indoor toilets and no running water. Everyone had had to use the one overfull outhouse behind the school. Those students told the rest of the team how awful those outhouses smelled. Even years later, they remembered that stench and how unfair it was that their White neighbors went to elementary schools with plumbing and heat and far more.

John Stokes described his friend Jack, a White boy whose family had moved from Canada into a house near the Stokeses' home. Jack and John became good friends, and Jack was upset when he realized that his school was much, much better than the Black school. He couldn't understand why there were separate schools for Black and White children in the first place. John, young at the time, couldn't explain it. When Jack asked John, "Why don't they want you to learn?" John didn't have an answer to that, either. But he thought about it a lot. By the time he and the strike committee met in early 1951, he'd come to the conclusion that the "White power structure was programming us to fail." Why? Why would anyone want a whole group of people to fail? John reasoned that White leaders wanted young Black people to fail when it came to an education and skills because that would keep all the good jobs, nice houses, and political power for the young White men and women.[17] It was an ugly truth. And by his senior year of high school, it was a truth that John Stokes was ready to challenge. He was proud to help with the strike.

Barbara told her team to keep the plans secret from teachers and the principal. They couldn't know anything about the strike. For one thing, they might stop it before it started. But she also feared that if the school board thought any teachers or administrators knew about or supported the strike, they'd be fired. And the one very good thing at Moton High School was the faculty and staff. They deserved protection, so this had to be completely student-run.

Dorothy Johnson Vaughan

Most Americans did not go to school after the eighth grade in the 1920s. Many Black children had to quit school even earlier, but Dorothy Johnson earned a degree in mathematics at nineteen. She moved to Virginia and became a math and French teacher at R. R. Moton High. She continued teaching after her marriage to Howard Vaughan Jr., and while raising their six children. Johnson Vaughan left Moton High School in 1943 to work as one of the first Black mathematicians at the National Advisory Committee for Aeronautics (NACA). Johnson Vaughan led a group of Black women mathematicians known as *computers* (Black and White mathematicians were segregated as were men and women). Segregation at the agency ended in 1958 when NACA became NASA (the National Aeronautics and Space Administration). Johnson Vaughan said that during segregation, "I changed what I could, and what I couldn't, I endured." A self-taught expert in computer programming languages, Johnson Vaughan worked on the mission that launched John Glenn into orbit in

1962. Dorothy Johnson Vaughan died in 2008 at the age of 98. She and her colleagues later gained recognition with the book and movie *Hidden Figures*.[18]

The committee continued meeting secretly through the early spring. They planned everything to the last detail, even checking the weather forecast to be sure the day of the strike would be dry. They couldn't ask four hundred students to stand in the rain, four hundred students who still didn't know they were going to go on strike. As the appointed date drew near, Barbara and the others felt confident that the plan would work.

On Monday morning, April 23, 1951, a committee member called Principal Jones on the telephone. Using his most adult voice, the boy told the principal that some Moton students were in trouble in town. The committee members were sure Jones would come to get the truant students and find out what they'd done. That's exactly what happened.

Once Jones left the school, other committee members delivered notes to each teacher saying there was an emergency assembly in the auditorium. The notes were signed "B. J." Teachers assumed that was Boyd Jones, the principal. The committee knew it was really Barbara Johns.

The committee members then hurried to the stage and sat behind the curtain. Once all the classes had crowded into the small auditorium, senior class president John Stokes quieted the room and led everyone in the Pledge of Allegiance. So far, it was a normal assembly. But when another member of the committee stood and asked the teachers to leave, everyone wondered what was going on. Most teachers trusted the students. They'd taught these young people to think for themselves, and now it seemed they were doing just that. The teachers left the auditorium. A pair of football players made sure any hesitant teacher left.

Barbara's younger sister, Joan, had come into the auditorium with all the other students, expecting to see Principal Jones onstage. When Barbara walked to the podium and began speaking, Joan was shocked. She slid down in her chair, afraid to find out what her sister was going to say. But as Barbara explained her idea for a strike and the reasons for it, Joan realized that the whole student body was listening closely. They were surprised that the girl they knew as pleasant and quiet was now fierce. Joan could have told them how determined Barbara was when she'd made up her mind to do something.

Barbara told the students that they had to stand together if anything was ever going to change. Could there be change? Barbara's confidence was contagious. Enthusiasm bubbled through the room, and soon students started singing pep songs and shouting cheers. They stood and clapped and stomped and roared their approval. John Stokes wrote later, "It was like a heavy thunderstorm in full force."[19]

Then the students—all of them—walked out in a strike against racism.

The young people of R. R. Moton High School had done just what Barbara had planned. They didn't see themselves as part of a big movement—this was 1951, several years before Rosa Parks or Central High School in Little Rock, Arkansas, or other widely known civil rights actions. The Moton students didn't break the law or do any damage. They didn't make threats. But there in quiet Prince Edward County, Virginia, Barbara Johns and the other students of R. R. Moton High School used their constitutional rights to free speech and assembly to demand change. They led the way.

CHAPTER 4

GOING BIGGER

1951–1954

Reverend L. Francis Griffin was a sturdy-looking young man with a deep crease across the bridge of his nose and laugh lines at the corners of his eyes. He seemed to move and speak slowly, but he had enough energy for three people. He'd spent much of his childhood in Farmville, Virginia, playing with both Black and White children on the empty lot next to the Griffin house and going to the county's Black schools. He left Farmville before graduating from Moton High School and worked in New York and North Carolina. Then he served in an all-Black tank battalion during World War II. After the war, he finished high school and went to college to study for the ministry. When his father, a pastor in Farmville, fell ill in 1949, he came back to help out for a while.[20]

Francis Griffin noticed right away that very little had changed in Farmville in the years he'd been away. Both Black and White people recognized him and asked how he'd been. That's the way it was in Prince Edward County. Polite, friendly, pleasant—but segregated. However, Griffin

Rev. L. Francis Griffin, pastor of Farmville's First Baptist Church and a strong supporter of the 1951 R. R. Moton High School strike.

noticed the character of the place more in 1949 than he had as a child. The world and the United States were changing after World War II.

Why hadn't that change come to his hometown? Perhaps that was one reason that he didn't plan to stay in Prince Edward. He wanted to settle somewhere new.

Sadly, the older Griffin didn't recover from his illness. He died not long after his son's return, and the younger man put his dreams on hold to take over as pastor of the First Baptist Church in Farmville—temporarily. The young pastor Griffin soon gained a reputation for challenging segregation loudly and openly in his sermons. That wasn't something his congregation was used to hearing, and some members weren't too sure how they felt about it. But no one doubted L. Francis Griffin's sincerity.

• • •

When Griffin heard about the Moton High School strike that morning in April 1951, he wanted to do whatever he could for the students. Their action was the kind of thing he'd been preaching about. He told the strike leaders they could hold meetings at the First Baptist Church, and they accepted.

In addition to his job as a church pastor, Griffin was the head of the Prince Edward County chapter of the NAACP (the organization that had been fighting for Black Americans' rights since 1909) in Virginia. He knew that lawyers working for the NAACP in Richmond had taken on cases involving school equality. They'd had some success. Barbara Johns and Carrie Stokes knew about the NAACP too, and got to work contacting those lawyers in Richmond.

Strike leaders also drew up a paper for strikers to take home to their parents and neighbors. They hoped that most parents would sign to show their support for the students' demands. Mr. and Mrs. Stokes approved of the strike, and were proud of what their children were doing. But the father of another strike leader thought the risk was too big. Barbara Johns's mother was away at work at the time, so she went to her grandmother. Later Barbara's grandmother said news of the strike and Barbara's role in it "took my breath away." But she gave her support when she saw how serious her granddaughter was. Barbara's father wasn't as sure, but didn't object. "My father says he is never surprised at anything I do," Barbara explained.[21] Many parents, though, were torn between pride and fear.

Reverend Griffin knew that some parents would hesitate or refuse to support the strike. Soon after he met with the students, he borrowed a car and drove all over the county talking to parents and community leaders in person since many did not have phones. He knocked on doors throughout the late afternoon and evening. At two in the morning, he was still knocking on doors to get support for the strike. And in many cases, he found parents and students still up discussing what was happening.[22]

The next day, attorney Oliver Hill in Richmond got a letter signed by Barbara Johns and Carrie Stokes.

> *Gentlemen,*
> *We hate to impose as we are doing, but . . . we have to ask for your help. . . . This morning, April 23, 1951, the students refused to attend class under any circumstances. You know that this is a very serious matter because we are out of school. . . . Please we beg you to come down. . . . We will provide a place for you to stay* [hotels did not rent rooms to Black people].[23]

Hill and Spottswood Robinson, both Black lawyers with the NAACP in Virginia, agreed to meet with the student strike leaders. They drove the sixty-five miles from Richmond to Farmville on Wednesday morning, planning to meet with the student leaders, listen to what they had to say, advise them to go back to school, and then drive on to another meeting. They admired the young people's nerve in striking, but students had never asked them for assistance before—it was always parents or school officials. And the two lawyers already had more cases than most attorneys could manage.

However, when Hill and Robinson got to the basement of the First Baptist Church, they found the hall filled with students and some parents. Barbara Johns and the others impressed them with their planning and determination, and the lawyers thought about taking the case after all. Oliver Hill said, "They handled themselves so well and their morale was so high that we didn't have the heart to say no. We said if their parents would support them, we would back them up."[24] However, there was a catch.

The students had gone on strike to demand better conditions at Moton High School, and that's what many of their parents had agreed to support. But the NAACP no longer sued school districts over inequality. They'd learned that winning those lawsuits never actually resulted in real improvements in Black schools. The organization had

decided to sue for an end to segregation in schools instead—
to sue to end "separate but equal" from the 1896 Supreme
Court decision. The lawyers would argue that segregated
schools were unequal and that this inequality violated the
Fourteenth Amendment. The NAACP could represent the
Moton students, Hill and Robinson told the strike leaders,
only if the students agreed to demand *desegregation*.

Fourteenth Amendment

Congress passed the Fourteenth Amendment in
June 1866. It became part of the US Constitution
after ratification by the states in 1868. Over time,
the Fourteenth Amendment—in particular section
one—has proved to be one of the Constitution's
most significant amendments. First, it answered
questions that the original Constitution did not. Section one of the amendment defines a citizen of the
United States as any person born or naturalized in
the United States and under US jurisdiction (at the
time, the foreign officials in the United States and
their children, even those born in the US, were not
under US authority). Second, section one says that
states cannot make any law that restricts the rights
of a US citizen. It goes on to say that all citizens in
all states must have the legal rights guaranteed in

the Constitution and that laws must apply equally to
every citizen. Third, the amendment gives Congress
the power to enforce these provisions. As more
states blocked Black citizens from exercising their
constitutional rights, lawyers for Black Americans
based their lawsuits on the promises and guarantees
of the Fourteenth Amendment. Many civil rights lawsuits today still rely on the Fourteenth Amendment.

That stunned Barbara and the others. They hadn't considered desegregation, and the idea of it frightened them.
Barbara said later, "It never entered my mind. . . . We didn't
know of such things."[25] Even so, after a long discussion
and a very close vote, the strike committee accepted the
NAACP's offer. Would their parents support a desegregation lawsuit too?

Students, parents, and community leaders met on Thurs-
day night. Hundreds and hundreds of people crammed
into the Moton building and spilled outside the doors.
Most of the parents were proud of their children for
standing up to inequality. But that didn't stop them from
being nervous and worried. Especially about demanding
desegregation.

Some parents believed that children had no business
making demands of adults at all. There was an expression

at the time: "Children should be seen and not heard." Others approved of the students speaking up, but they weren't sure desegregation was a good idea. Like the students, Moton parents admired Principal Jones. According to Reverend Griffin, "Jones's school was the most democratic thing that ever happened among the Negroes around here. His students . . . were taught to think for themselves and criticize and ask questions."[26] Would that happen in a nonsegregated school? Would Black students be able to raise their hands and express their opinions? Or would they find themselves pushed aside? Would someone like John or Carrie Stokes be elected president of the class? Or would that honor automatically go to a White student?

There's a difference between desegregation and integration. It's one thing to end segregation, to *de-segregate*, and put Black and White students in the same school. But if Black students or other students of color aren't part of the school community in every way, with all the same opportunities and experiences as White students, it's not *integration*. If students of color can't see their culture, their traditions, and their values as part of the school culture, it's not integration. And students at Moton had received a very good education despite the hardships.

Moton teachers had earned tremendous respect from parents and students. For one thing, they had found ways to work around the terrible conditions at the school. But

that was only part of it. Those teachers were well educated and dedicated to giving their students the skills
they'd need to survive and succeed in a world filled with
obstacles. They'd taught their students to be proud of who
they were. They'd taught them Black history and the real
meaning of "all men are created equal." They'd taught
them the power of education. They were models for using
hard work, bright minds, and skill to overcome the odds.
Would White teachers who might not want to teach
Black students be as good? If the schools desegregated,
the school board certainly wouldn't hire any Black teacher,
no matter how well qualified. Black students could lose as
much as they gained.

While parents may have disagreed on the desegregation
lawsuit, though, they all agreed that county leaders and
other White residents were likely to retaliate for the Black
students' actions and demands. Black-owned businesses
might suffer. White employers might fire the parents
of the striking students. White county residents could
retaliate in a hundred other ways. One student said, "The
children got so far ahead of the parents, they didn't have
anything to say to us."[27] Perhaps those parents had more
to fear. Barbara Johns, though, was impressed with the
parents' gradual acceptance as they got used to the idea.
"They were at first bewildered by it all—but they attended

the meetings in full strength. . . . They stood behind us—timidly at first but firmly," she wrote later.[28]

Hundreds of Black families met again, this time at the First Baptist Church. Several community leaders spoke in favor of joining the NAACP lawsuit. But a former principal of the school criticized the student leaders and the NAACP lawyers. Barbara Johns jumped from her seat near the podium and took control of the meeting and the crowd. She told people to ignore the former principal—he was too willing to go along with White leaders to avoid trouble. As normally quiet, reserved, and polite as she was, Barbara raised her voice and called the man a traitor to his people. Suddenly the crowded room erupted in cheering and applause. John Stokes wrote, "She was no longer just a 16-year-old student. She became a Superstar, an instant heroine."[29] Over two hundred people signed the petition to sue Prince Edward County.

The students agreed that they would return to school on Monday, May 7. By then, they and their parents had already felt early reaction to the strike. On the Sunday morning before the students went back to school, someone erected a ten-foot-high wooden cross in the schoolyard and set it on fire. The Ku Klux Klan was known to frighten and intimidate Black people with cross burnings. But the police called the burning cross a prank, not the work of the KKK, and did not investigate. No one was surprised. It was true that Prince Edward County had never had a lot of Klan activity before, but then, they'd never had Black students suing to desegregate the schools before. Whatever the truth was, Black residents had no choice but to hope the police were right and watch out for themselves and each other.

Black families quickly took precautions since many lived in farmhouses far from neighbors and couldn't count on the police for help. Like other rural families, John and Carrie Stokes's parents owned shotguns and a .22-caliber rifle. They loaded all of them, just in case. Whenever their dogs barked at night over the next few weeks, they turned off the lights and took up their weapons. The fear was terrible.[30]

Nothing else happened right away. Most White county residents hadn't shown any open response to the strike. But everyone knew it would come. On May 8, 1951, the day after the students returned to school, an opinion piece in Prince Edward County's newspaper, the *Farmville Herald*, said,

> Instead of a local effort to improve school conditions, the movement has become a movement to eliminate racial segregation from the Virginia Constitution.
>
> We regret that Prince Edward was chosen for this test case on segregation. . . . The progress of

the South . . . of any place where two races must live together, depends upon the principles of segregation. . . . Until this incident, the leaders of the races in Prince Edward County have worked together for the benefit of each. Local problems have been discussed and resolved by co-operation and understanding. . . . If ever a united front, a happy people, a determined effort to preserve our way of life was needed, it is today.[31]

Think about those words. Did Black residents of Prince Edward County really agree that a leaky, cold, damp, poorly equipped school was "for the benefit" of their children while White children had good facilities? Did White residents believe that? And what, exactly, did "*our* way of life" mean? *Whose* way of life?

In late May, the NAACP filed a lawsuit in federal court—*Davis v. County School Board of Prince Edward County*. In June, the school board fired R. R. Moton principal M. Boyd Jones, saying that he hadn't kept the students "under control." Black farmers suddenly found some of their White customers going elsewhere, and White-owned banks refused loans to longtime Black clients. No one in the Black community was surprised. They had known there would be retaliation for suing the county.[32]

The US Court System

Legal conflicts in the United States are decided in courts of law. Those courts interpret the law—say what the law means—and then apply it to the particular case. State courts deal with state laws and issues. Federal courts deal with federal or national laws and constitutional issues. Criminal cases deal with people accused of breaking the law and the punishment of a person found guilty. Civil cases settle disagreements. A disagreement may involve a contract, or a question of responsibility for an automobile accident, or other issues. Civil cases can also involve violations of constitutional rights. In a civil case, the person or group bringing a complaint against another person or group is the plaintiff. When the plaintiff asks the court to hear the complaint, the plaintiff is said to be filing suit or suing. The person or group defending itself against the complaint is the defendant.

At the same time, several White business and community leaders told Black leaders that the county was already planning new schools for Black children. That wasn't news—supposed plans for improving Black schools had been empty promises for years. The White leaders said that if Black parents dropped the NAACP lawsuit, the county would replace R. R. Moton High School with a brand-new, bigger school. Reverend Griffin was at the meeting and stopped the White men in their tracks. He talked about segregation as evil and said, "I didn't come here to sell my people down the river." At that point, according to Griffin, the meeting "just fizzled out."[33] There was no going back.

Oliver Hill and Spottswood Robinson appeared in federal court in February 1952, nine months after they filed the NAACP lawsuit (scheduling court cases can take a very long time). *Davis v. County School Board of Prince Edward County* was named for Dorothy Davis, a Moton student whose name was printed first on the list of students and families filing suit. Hill and Robinson asked the court to strike down (get rid of) the Virginia Constitution's requirement for segregation in public schools. They argued that the requirement violated the US Constitution's Fourteenth Amendment, the amendment that guarantees equality under the law. Segregated schools were not equal because they treated one group of students differently from another group. All the while, the county school board pressed ahead with plans for a new Black high school. Board members wanted to prove that they took the "equal" part of "separate but equal" seriously. But they made no plans for the elementary schools and their smelly outhouses.

People in the county continued to be polite to one another despite the tension. Many student leaders, including the Stokes twins, had graduated from Moton the previous spring and moved away for college or jobs. It was easy to pretend nothing had happened. Barbara Johns was now a high school senior, but she wasn't at R. R. Moton High School. Her family had feared for her safety after a friendly White neighbor had come to warn them that Barbara was in danger. Quietly, secretly, they'd sent her to live with her uncle Vernon Johns in Montgomery, Alabama. Even her closest friends didn't know where she was until much later.

Imagine starting senior year as the new student in a strange school far from friends and closest family. Then imagine doing that under orders to tell no one there or back home what had happened. It was a big price to pay for standing up for equality. But if the NAACP lawyers won the lawsuit . . .

They didn't. The federal court in Virginia ruled against the NAACP and the students. In looking at the separation of White and Black children in Prince Edward County, the court recognized that the county had discriminated against Black children. But then the three-judge panel said, "We have found no hurt or harm to either race,"[34] since Black students in the county were going to get a new high school. True, that's what Barbara and the others had decided to strike for in the first place. But their dreams had expanded. They had dared to imagine real change. And now their dreams might be over. All that work, all that hope and worry . . .

Construction started on the new R. R. Moton High School. Principal Jones left Virginia to go to graduate school, and Barbara Johns finished high school in Alabama in the spring of 1952. Life went on, and so did the NAACP. Attorneys Oliver Hill and Spottswood Robinson weren't ready to accept defeat. They appealed the federal court ruling (requested a new hearing) to the United States Supreme Court, the nation's highest court.

Good news came that fall when the Supreme Court agreed to hear the Prince Edward County, Virginia, appeal in *Davis v. County School Board of Prince Edward County* along with four other appeals on school segregation. The other cases came from South Carolina, Delaware, the District of Columbia (Washington, DC), and Kansas. Together they became known as *Brown v. Board of Education of Topeka*, the first case on the list of five. Arguments began in December 1952.

It took a year and a half, but on May 17, 1954, the US Supreme Court issued its opinion in *Brown v. Board of Education*. It had been three long, hard years since the Moton High School students had voted to sue for desegregation, and two years since they'd lost in federal court. Now, in a unanimous decision, the nine Supreme Court justices concluded that "in the field of public education the doctrine of 'separate but equal' has no place. Separate educational facilities are inherently [naturally] unequal." The appeals were finished. The court case was over. Segregation in America's public schools was unconstitutional.

When the ruling came, Barbara Johns was a student at Spelman College, and John Stokes was at Virginia State University. At last, they and their fellow Moton students had won their case in a *landmark* decision—a decision with enormous significance for the future of the whole country. They could be proud that their part of the case was the only student-led lawsuit. And 75 percent of the plaintiffs (the people making the complaint) in *Brown v. Board* were Prince Edward County students. Young Black students in Prince Edward County had won a victory for every Black child in the United States. Or so it seemed.

In reality, the battle for desegregation had just begun.

CHAPTER 5

MASSIVE RESISTANCE

1954–1959

H eadlines all over the country shouted the news: SCHOOL SEGREGATION IS UNCONSTITUTIONAL; SCHOOL SEGREGATION BANNED. In Virginia, segregationists felt shock. Was the fight really over? Harry Flood Byrd, Sr. didn't think so. He wasn't about to give in.

Just about everyone in Virginia knew who Harry Flood Byrd was. A millionaire. A politician. Brother of Richard Byrd, the famous admiral and South Pole explorer. The legendary Byrd family could trace their Virginia roots back to John Rolfe and Pocahontas in Jamestown. Harry Byrd kept close watch on the five thousand acres of apple orchards that made him rich, but his real passion was politics. He'd been a state senator in the 1920s and then Virginia's governor. In 1954, he was in his twenty-first year as a United States senator.

On the day the Supreme Court issued its ruling on school segregation, Senator Byrd wrote, "Instead of promoting the education of our children, it [the decision] will have the opposite effect."[35] In other words, desegregation

US Senator Harry Flood Byrd, Sr., called for "massive resistance" to school desegregation through state laws that included punishing schools that acted to integrate after the 1954 Supreme Court decision declaring segregation in public schools unconstitutional.

would harm children's schooling. His opinion wasn't surprising. Harry Byrd had been defending segregation throughout his life.

White people in Prince Edward County paid attention to Byrd. They also paid attention to local voices, including J. Barrye Wall. Raised in Prince Edward, Wall had grown up in Prince Edward and had been the owner and publisher of the *Farmville Herald* newspaper for thirty years. He was a lifelong segregationist just as Byrd was. Wall published his newspaper for White readers and used it as a microphone to make his views known through his editorial or opinion pieces (Black residents usually read the *Richmond Afro-American*, a Black-owned paper).

Days after the news of the Brown ruling, Wall wrote "We believe . . . Negroes would be as reluctant to receive whites into their schools as is the case with the whites," and finished, "This newspaper continues its firm belief in the principles of segregation in public schools . . . We believe it is in the best interests of all our people."[36]

Senator Byrd and J. Barrye Wall spoke of Black and White Virginians working together in cooperation. They referred to "our children" or "all our people" and seemed to assume that Black citizens either agreed with them, or didn't care. They'd always thought and talked and written this way just as most members of Prince Edward's all-White school board and all-White board of supervisors did. But they didn't say *why* they thought they could speak for Black men and women whose lives were so different from theirs—people who faced daily restrictions and discrimination that White people, particularly wealthy White people, had never faced for a single minute. Had Byrd and Wall asked their Black neighbors for their opinions on segregation, education, or anything else? They probably thought they didn't need to.

Like their Black neighbors, many of Prince Edward's White residents had long, long family ties to the region. But White residents had been taught from their earliest years that White people were superior to Black people— smarter, more capable, more mature, more hardworking, even more moral. They'd been told that White men should be the decision-makers in government, business, and society. That Black people could not succeed on their own and needed help. In short, they had learned the ideas of White supremacy. White residents and their parents and grandparents had been looking at Farmville's Confederate Soldier Monument since 1900. Many had accepted that statue's message of White power. During the 1950s, their children and grandchildren saw that monument every day and learned history from school textbooks that lied. That's right. Their textbooks told lies.

In the late 1940s, White supremacists in Virginia pushed for schoolbooks that taught from their viewpoint, not from the evidence. The new books presented an inaccurate version of history promoted by White supremacist politicians and organizations, including the United

The Virginia Defenders of State Sovereignty Confederate Soldier Monument in Farmville, Virginia was erected in 1900. The statue was removed in 2020.

Daughters of the Confederacy. That was the group that also raised money for many Confederate statues.

As a result of their efforts, one middle school history book in Virginia showed a drawing of an African family, all well-dressed in European-style clothing, being welcomed with a handshake by their new enslaver. Is that how enslaved people arrived in Virginia? The book claimed that slavery had been "an educational process" for Black people, and that during the American Civil War, enslaved men and women had *chosen* to stay on plantations and "supported the war unanimously."[37] What about the hundreds of thousands of enslaved people who'd escaped to US Army camps and freedom? Or the 180,000 Black men who'd risked execution to flee plantations and join the US Army?

One author of books like these worried that earlier books misled children by saying that slavery caused a war in 1861. Misled? What about the words of the secessionist leaders in 1861? What had they said to cause them to secede?

A false and misleading illustration showing an African family arriving in Virginia, well-dressed, with luggage, and warmly welcomed by their so-called "master," their enslaver. The image appeared in Virginia textbooks used across the state for many years. It and the text gave thousands of school children a vastly distorted view of slavery in America.

Mississippi's declaration of secession stated, "Our position is thoroughly identified with the institution of slavery—the greatest material interest of the world." Texas leaders wrote, "The servitude of the African race, as existing in these States, is mutually beneficial to both bond [enslaved] and free, and . . . justified by the revealed will of the Almighty Creator. . . ." That's a mouthful, but it meant that slavery in the Southern states was good for both Black and White people, enslaved and free, and that God approved of it. Georgia's declaration said that the "reason [for secession] was [the North's] fixed purpose to limit, restrain, and finally abolish slavery in the States where it exists."[38]

It's true that some seceding states listed other reasons for their choice as well. But the textbooks' authors had no excuse for ignoring or not knowing or denying the whole truth. The people promoting the inaccurate version of history in the new textbooks—including members of the United Daughters of the Confederacy—may have believed what those books said because it was what they had learned in childhood. But declarations of secession, papers, letters, legal documents, photographs, and eyewitness accounts prove them wrong.

The same author who worried about children being misled said that the "primary function of history is to build patriotism."[39] Read those words again. Did the author mean that we *don't* study history to learn what actually happened in the past? Or that it's okay to make things up if the truth is ugly? Does it mean that we should hide the parts of the past that are painful in order to feel good about our country? That we can't feel proud of a country that faces its past and tries to do better?

Prominent White Virginians like J. Barrye Wall openly admitted their racist beliefs. They weren't ashamed of the way they thought and felt. But they saw Virginia's White supremacy as different from the White supremacy in other parts of the South. They saw it as better. They weren't Ku Klux Klansmen or anything like Klansmen, they said. They didn't hate anyone or wish anyone harm. They pointed with pride to the state's tradition of good manners, polite words, and some kindness toward everyone—including political opponents and Black people. They called it "the Virginia way," and they discouraged racial violence and open hatred. They claimed that they simply wanted to keep the races separate.

Perhaps they thought that the pleasant hellos and friendly bits of conversation between White and Black neighbors in places like Farmville were proof that both White and Black residents were content. Perhaps they saw the lack of constant violence against the Black community as a gift of sorts. After all, when a Black person in Prince Edward County forgot his "place" and made too many demands, his White boss might fire him, but it wasn't likely that a gang of White men would beat or lynch him, as happened elsewhere. The way White leaders saw it, Black people in Prince Edward should be grateful.

Prince Edward County and the rest of Virginia may have seen fewer murders of Black residents than many other places. But there were very real threats and attacks. John Stokes knew that when he tore through barbed wire to hide. Barbara Johns knew that when her parents sent her to Alabama. Those threats and attacks usually went unreported because the victims were afraid to say anything and understood that the all-White police force wouldn't make any arrests anyway.

Would Barbara Johns have been harmed if her parents hadn't sent her away in 1951? There's no way to know. But not long after the 1954 *Brown* decision, the Johnses' house burned to the ground in a suspicious fire. "There was nothing left at all," Barbara's sister, Joan, said. "Just ashes." Barbara didn't live there anymore, and thankfully, the family wasn't home at the time. Still, they lost everything. "It had to be arson," Joan said. But local White officials never made an arrest.[40] The Virginia way's pleasant words and smiles didn't investigate arson. Arson or not, the Johns family couldn't afford to rebuild their house and left Prince Edward County to live in Washington, DC.

Could White leaders explain why Mr. and Mrs. Johns should be grateful?

Wall and Prince Edward County officials pointed to the new Moton High School as another reason why the county's Black residents should be grateful. Some Virginia counties had no high schools for Black students at all. And certainly, Black parents and students were relieved to have a new high school in place of the tar paper shacks. But grateful? Black residents like Reverend Griffin had gone to every school board meeting, month after month for years, to pressure White board members. The construction had started only when the school board had realized that a new high school for Black students might keep the courts from ordering the county to desegregate. No matter what Wall and the others said about the new school, they missed the point.

Even if the county's all-White school board had supplied the Black high school with new textbooks instead of discards from the White school, even if they had provided new cleats for the football team instead of used shoes from the White football players, even if they had built decent elementary schools with bathrooms and heat . . . even if they had done all of that and more, Black residents would have had no reason to be *grateful* to them.[41]

Prince Edward's Black community didn't want "favors" from "kind-hearted" White men. They didn't "owe" White leaders anything. They were citizens and taxpayers just as White citizens were. And they didn't want to be treated as less than that. Nice manners and one new school after years of asking wasn't the answer. The answer was real equality.

The Supreme Court hadn't set any deadlines for integrating schools in its 1954 ruling. Most states in the far South went on operating their schools the way they always had while they waited for the courts to force them to do something else. School officials in Maryland, Delaware, Kentucky, and other states, however, began serious work on plans for integration. So did officials in some Virginia counties.

Prominent White men in Prince Edward County organized and made plans too. But they weren't school officials, and they weren't planning for integration. Instead, J. Barrye Wall and other influential men formed the Defenders of State Sovereignty and Individual Liberties—Defenders, for short. The name came from an inscription on the Confederate monument in Farmville. Over six hundred White county residents joined the organization. Other prominent White men followed their lead and formed chapters around the state. The Defenders in Prince Edward and in other counties planned to keep schools segregated no matter what the Supreme Court said. The same was true in other Southern states. When the court ordered schools to move forward on desegregation "with all deliberate speed" in May 1955, the Defenders had their plans ready.

The first step was to ask the courts to give the county the time to make any changes. A lot of time. That was easy enough since it really would take time to reorganize all the schools in the county. Many school districts had asked for and received postponements. They wouldn't have to desegregate for the 1955–56 school year.

The second step was to start a private school. The Supreme Court's decision applied only to *public* education—schools paid for with taxpayer money. So all over the South, White parents who wanted to avoid segregated schools got busy setting up private "segregation academies" that didn't have to follow the Supreme Court's ruling. Prince Edward County's leaders planned to do the same thing. They started a foundation, and well-off parents and business owners made donations and pledged more donations for the future. The Defenders put pressure on White residents who didn't contribute right away. The money began to come in.

Contributions, however, wouldn't be enough to cover the academy's costs. So the third step was to find ways to use local and state tax money for the Prince Edward Academy. Government support for a private school? Do governments do that? In Prince Edward, the Defenders convinced county officials to stop collecting taxes for public schools if the court enforced desegregation. Once White parents didn't have to pay those taxes, they could use the money they saved to pay for the private school. The Defenders also worked to *amend* or change, the state constitution and state law. The changes would allow them to give White parents money for private school tuition using state tax money. And many politicians around the state were very happy to support the changes. Think about that.

The plan wasn't unique in Virginia or the rest of the South. But Prince Edward's plan was particularly bold and became a model for segregationists across the South. And the Defenders had every reason to believe it would work—they had United States Senator Harry Byrd on their side.

Senator Byrd had already called on Southern states to stand together in "massive resistance" to the Supreme Court's decision on school segregation. He didn't ask for violence or rebellion. Instead he argued that states could ignore a federal action they believed was unconstitutional. He said that the federal government had no right to tell states how to run their schools or spend the tax money they collected. "I think that in time," he said, "the rest of the country will realize that racial integration is not going to be accepted in the South."[42] Can states really decide which federal laws are constitutional and which are not? Or whether to obey a Supreme Court order? Secessionists at the time of the Civil War argued that states could make those decisions. A hundred years later, Senator Harry Byrd made the same argument.

"Massive resistance" quickly became a battle cry across much of the Southern United States. Small, quiet Prince Edward County took the lead. Weeks later, the Prince Edward County Board of Supervisors issued a declaration signed by thousands of White county residents.

> We, the undersigned citizens of Prince Edward County, Virginia, hereby affirm our conviction [belief] that the separation of the races in the public schools of this County is absolutely necessary and do affirm that we prefer to abandon public schools and educate our children in some other way if that be necessary to preserve separation of the races in the schools of the County.[43]

Read that declaration again. Abandon public schools? The county would close them permanently. Educate their children in some other way? They'd set up a private, segregated school for White children and allow thousands of Black children and many poor White children to stop going to school entirely. Don't children have to go to school? The Defenders had state support to *repeal*— or get rid of—the law saying parents must educate their children. If this group succeeded in ending public education in Prince Edward, other school districts could do the same. One by one, counties and then states could choose to destroy public education in the United States.

Some White county residents disagreed with the Defenders' extreme ideas right from the start. That didn't mean they wanted integration. But they supported education for all children. They believed that the United States needed educated citizens in the workforce and in the military. They believed in free public education for everyone.

The Defenders were ready. Step four of their plan was to enforce White unity—no disagreement—on the issue of desegregation. They weren't going to put up with *dissent*—differing opinions. They had ways to keep White citizens in line just as they did Black citizens.

James Bash, the much-liked principal of the all-White Farmville High School believed in public education and said that he would never work for an organization set up to get around a Supreme Court ruling. Before long, many teachers at Farmville High School avoided him in the halls and ignored him as much as they could. Some neighbors did the same thing, snubbing him and his family. A local minister, James Kennedy, got a similar reaction when he spoke up. Within the year, both Bash and Kennedy resigned from their jobs and moved away. Dr. Gordon Moss, a professor at Longwood College in Farmville, also believed in public schools and said so. Like Bash and Kennedy, he soon lost friends and felt unwelcome at local businesses. A shopping center owner who agreed with Moss lost business as White customers boycotted his stores.[44] And school board members who wouldn't give in to everything the Defenders wanted also faced retaliation. The message to the rest of the White community was clear. Whites would stick together in opposition to desegregation and in support of closing the public schools or suffer consequences.

In the meantime, children in Prince Edward County continued to attend segregated schools as the county was granted one desegregation delay after another. They went through the 1955–56 school year and the 1956–57 school year and the school year after that. Segregationists made fiery speeches and wrote angry editorials defending themselves. But vague threats and intimidation couldn't stop the NAACP from fighting in the courts. Ignoring the loud voices, NAACP attorneys won cases in parts of Virginia and in other states. Court after court ordered school districts to obey the Supreme Court's ruling.

Finally, in May 1959—five years after *Brown v. Board of Education* and eight years after the Moton High School strike—a federal appeals court ruled that Prince Edward County had to begin desegregating its public schools that

September. No more excuses, no more delays. By then, small numbers of Black students had entered previously all-White schools in Norfolk and Arlington, as well as in Front Royal and Charlottesville, Virginia. There was little serious trouble.

The same thing had happened in other parts of the South, though some communities did experience serious violence. But despite court rulings, progress toward integration was horribly slow in some places and almost non-existent in most others. Segregation academies continued to spring up, especially where Black students would out-number White students in desegregated schools. Some districts even closed their schools for a time. But the courts were on the side of desegregation. Surely, massive resistance couldn't work forever. White supremacists saw it differently.

The 1959 court decision mandating desegregation by September was the moment the Defenders of State Sovereignty and Individual Liberties had been waiting for. They assured parents that the Prince Edward Academy would be up and running by September. There was no building yet, but leaders made arrangements to hold classes in church basements and Sunday school class-rooms, at the Moose Club Lodge and the Women's Club Hall. Volunteers put makeshift desks together as officials hired teachers and administrators.[45]

There was no gym, of course, or science labs. No art,

or music, or foreign language classes. No library or cafeteria. Not enough books or supplies for the academy's 1,446 students.[46] Farmville High School had had all those things. Did the academy's shortcomings sound a lot like the problems at the old R. R. Moton High School? The problems that had pushed Black students to strike? That didn't matter to the Defenders. What mattered was that Prince Edward Academy did not have to admit Black students.

Less than a month after the order to integrate, the Prince Edward County Board of Supervisors announced that it would provide no money at all for the county's public schools in the coming year. None. "It is with the most profound regret that we have been compelled [forced] to take this action."[47] Compelled? Forced? By what?

Longwood Professor Gordon Moss called the move "unintentional evil." A group of local Black ministers said it was "contrary to the simple laws of decency, the American ideal of democracy, the Christian concept of justice, and the moral law of God."[48]

No one on the board listened. About 1,700 Black students and some poor White students were out of luck. All twenty county schools stood closed, locked, abandoned. Most White children would go to the new academy, many with financial aid. And Black children? As of September 1959, Prince Edward's Black students were literally locked out of school, and there were no plans for them at all.

CHAPTER 6

SHATTERED DREAMS

1959–1961

S ix-year-old Ricky Brown had been waiting to start school forever. At least it seemed that way. Going to school would mean that he was smart. That he was one of the big kids. He and his cousin loved watching the noisy, yellow school buses that rattled by every morning and afternoon. The boys made up songs about those buses and tried to imagine how important the older children must feel climbing aboard. Now it was supposed to be Ricky's turn to climb onto that bus with the older kids.

"I was very excited about going to the first grade, but the bus never came for me," he said years later. "I got dressed the first day of school and after the bus didn't come, my mother tried to explain to me what happened. Being six years old, I couldn't really understand what she was telling me."[49] The bus didn't come for Ricky the next day either. Or the day after that, and Ricky Brown's heart nearly broke. Why didn't the bus come? Ricky had been waiting and waiting and finally, he was old enough. He wanted to go to school.

Shirley Jackson lived near Ricky Brown. She'd finished

first grade in June and spent the summer playing with her sisters Patricia and Elizabeth and their friends. They collected soda bottles and turned them in for money so they could buy ice cream (bottle deposits were an early form of recycling). They talked about the new clothes their mother had gotten them for the coming school year and what they would wear on the first day. Like a lot of other Black parents in Prince Edward County, Shirley's mother had to work hard to give her six children new clothes for school. But new clothes showed that school was important. She wanted her children to understand that.

Mrs. Jackson didn't have much schooling herself, and she earned money by cleaning and ironing for White families. Those families weren't rich, but they could afford to hire someone to do their housework. They could buy their children plenty of new clothes and shoes. They had cars and nice furniture. In short, they had more money than the Jackson family would ever have, and their children had more opportunities. Education could give the Jackson children the chance their mother had never had.

When September came, Shirley and her brother and sisters left their house in a good mood, excited to head back to Mary E. Branch Elementary School No. 1. Who would be in their classes? Were there any new teachers this year? They talked and joked and laughed as they walked down the street. But when they got close to the school, they stopped. Where were all the other kids? Why wasn't the schoolyard filled with children lining up and teachers giving them instructions? They saw only a handful of their schoolmates. Worried, they went to the door and found heavy chains around the handles and a big lock holding them tight. A small number of teachers with sad, serious faces came over. There would be no school that day, they said. The school was closed and would stay that way.

The children started back the way they'd come, but there was no laughing or joking now. Shirley started crying and couldn't stop. She was supposed to be in second grade. Her sisters cried with her. Their school was chained shut like an old, abandoned building. They felt abandoned too. What were they supposed to do? They needed to go to school. "No one could explain the situation to help it make sense," Shirley said years later.[50]

Most Black families had heard the news of the school closings when officials had announced it in June. They'd gone to meetings to discuss it. Some parents tried to talk to their children about it, but many very young children couldn't believe it or didn't understand. Other parents kept quiet, hoping that the county would back down or that the state or federal government would step in during the summer. Surely the county couldn't really shut all the schools. Could it?

It wasn't just small children who felt the heartbreak that September, of course. Douglas Vaughan was set to start ninth grade when the schools closed. He'd grown up in a very poor section of Prince Edward County that he described as being "off-limits to Black and White people." He lived in the town of Farmville, but on Douglas's side of the railroad tracks, many streets were unpaved and without sidewalks. Some of the small, wooden houses lacked plumbing and had outhouses in the backyards.

Douglas and his brother and sisters lived with their grandmother, who was ill, and their mother, who became addicted to alcohol and couldn't take care of them. The children "raised each other," he said later. Their house had electricity and water, but they often lost both because they couldn't pay the bills. And while even fairly poor families tried to get each child a new outfit to start the school year, Douglas's only pair of shoes was worn out. "I learned to walk to keep the sole from flapping," he remembered.[51]

Missing out on a chance at education was terrible for any child. Imagine how terrible it was for students like Douglas Vaughan. They lost their schooling and their safe space— the place where they could put the worries and fears they faced at home out of their minds and be themselves. Be kids. Douglas described school as "a place where I could go and have friends and feel loved or liked."[52] Without school, he had no one to turn to and nowhere to go.

The school closings shattered dreams for older teens, too. Students expecting to start junior or senior year of

Deloris Blanton Hendricks, age eight. When the schools closed after her sophomore year of high school, Deloris went to live with her grandparents, whose house in Cumberland County had no plumbing or electricity. She graduated from high school there in 1961.

high school saw their futures evaporate. They'd worked hard to succeed and were on track to get a high school diploma. That would mean job opportunities or the possibility of college or trade school. Imagine being so close to reaching a goal and having it snatched away. All that effort for nothing. All those hopes and plans destroyed. "When you're seventeen, that's not real," one student said. "You can't conceive of the schools not opening."[53]

The Reverend Francis Griffin, still pastor of the First Baptist Church in Farmville, worried all summer about the school closings even as he told people that things would work out. He loved teaching and valued education (his own children teased that they couldn't find a place to sit in their house because there were books on every surface).

Griffin had always encouraged the county's Black teen-agers to finish high school no matter how hard it was or how tempting it was to take a job and make a little money instead of going to school. He knew if they left school, they'd probably never go back. And he believed that every child should finish school whether they wanted to be a doctor or work on the family farm. So, when Black residents of the county organized the Prince Edward County Christian Association (PECCA) to fight the school closings in court and help children get through the crisis, Griffin agreed to lead the organization.[54]

Francis Griffin had stayed in Prince Edward County because the church had needed him when his father had died. Now he stayed because the whole community needed him. Most Black people in Prince Edward liked and respected the pastor, though some, especially older people, disagreed with his push for desegregation.[55] They thought he was demanding too much too fast. But like Martin Luther King, Jr.; Vernon Johns; and others, Griffin believed that addressing issues of racism, inequality, and poverty was part of his duty and calling as a clergyman. And like King and the others, he paid a heavy price for speaking out.

After the Supreme Court ruled in *Brown v. Board* in 1954, many White county residents who had been friendly with Griffin, even White fellow ministers, turned against him. Some accused him of planning the strike—

something he always denied. Many despised the NAACP and criticized his participation in the organization. Before long, Griffin felt their anger in more concrete ways.

Reverend Griffin had never been very good at managing money, and with five young children, he often had debts at local stores. White store owners now insisted that he pay in cash. They would give him no more credit. That sometimes left the Griffin family without enough to eat and left the children with outgrown, worn clothing. Other business owners demanded that Griffin pay all of what he owed on loans. When he couldn't do that right away, they took back his car and the furniture he'd bought on credit. Whether they were punishing Reverend Griffin for causing trouble, or just trying to keep their businesses running, isn't certain. But Griffin believed their actions were retaliation, and they left his family in a terrible situation. Occasional threatening phone calls made things even worse. The pastor continued with his own church and accepted duties at small churches outside Prince Edward County to make extra money. He also took on a bigger role with the Virginia State Conference NAACP—one with a salary. He wasn't going to give in.[56]

In 1959, Griffin turned his immediate attention to finding help for students entering their junior or senior year of high school. He and Reverend Alexander Dunlap, a minister from the local African Methodist Episcopal (AME) Church, organized a program with a junior college about ninety miles south of Farmville in North Carolina. The AME church ran Kittrell Junior College and offered high school classes to a small number of students. The school agreed to accept about sixty Prince Edward County teens. Families paid one half of the usual tuition if they could afford that. PECCA raised the money for those who needed financial help.

Less than a week after the Prince Edward schools should have opened for the 1959 school year, cars started lining up outside the First Baptist Church in Farmville. Soon some twenty cars wound down the street and around the corner, all of them filled with nervous, excited Black teens and their parents. Just days earlier, the teens had been hoping schools in Prince Edward would open. Now their parents were about to drive them to North Carolina for school. It didn't seem real.

Marie Walton was in one of those cars. She was an excellent student and loved school. When she'd heard that the schools were closing, she thought her future was ruined. That she would be a dropout. It was horrifying. When she learned about the Kittrell program, she knew she had to go whether she was ready to leave home or not. Just a few days later, she told her family goodbye.[57]

Phyllistine Ward and her brother Ronnie and their

Phyllistine Ward, a high school junior, was one of sixty Prince Edward students who went to Kittrell Junior College in North Carolina to continue their education. She then went to Iowa through a student placement program for her senior year, where she lived with a Quaker family in the small, supportive town of Yellow Springs.

parents joined the parade of cars too. So did some of their cousins. Phyllistine later described the odd feeling of being a high school student on a college campus. The college instructors tried to put them at ease, and were ready to help them with their studies. But most of the teens were homesick. Reverend Dunlap helped ease the loneliness with weekly trips to Kittrell. On every visit, he delivered the care packages filled with baked goods and toiletries that parents packed for their children. But the students wanted the kind of high school experience they'd always imagined. They even asked for permission to hold a junior-senior prom on the college campus. Mostly, though, they focused on getting that diploma.[58]

Reverend Griffin visited Kittrell as often as he could, but there was much more to do at home, and he had his NAACP work as well. While the college program was wonderful, it reached only sixty students. That left over 1,600 students without schooling. He had to find ways to help them since it was clear that the county was not going to back down and reopen the schools anytime soon.

At the same time, many women in the Black community decided to do what they could for the children who had no schools. Several had been teachers or had more education than many other Black adults in Prince Edward. They opened their homes to students of various ages and offered lessons in reading and math. They used whatever materials they could find. Older students helped younger ones, and the classes met every day just as a regular school would have.

Flossie White ran a beauty parlor, but she decided to help out when the schools closed. "I had as many as fifty children in my basement," she recalled. "We had old chairs, old bus seats, and a few chairs from schools." They worked on English, math, and current events. She insisted that the students "read the newspaper and give a report each day." Mrs. White got books from the donations that people outside the county sent to Reverend Griffin. And she made sure the children went outdoors for daily exercise. Friday afternoons were reserved for dancing to Mrs. White's records. What about her regular job? "After the students left in the afternoon, I opened up my beauty parlor."[59]

PECCA organized additional informal schooling. By February 1960, the first of ten "training centers" opened around the county in church basements and community centers. They weren't real schools, and PECCA didn't pretend they were. Many of the adults who worked in the centers had no experience or training as teachers. One mother of five school-aged children agreed to help when Reverend Griffin asked. She and another woman organized classes in an old, run-down building that had once been a school. "Neither one of us was certified to teach," she explained, "but our presence in the classroom kept the children out of mischief and assisted them in learning."[60] The goal was to help children keep up with their reading and math skills and learn about citizenship and current events. The centers offered arts and crafts with donated materials, as well as time for exercise and play.

About six hundred students were able to take advantage of the centers over the next two years, some of them walking four or five miles each way. The training centers' volunteers hoped to keep those children from forgetting what they'd learned in school, but the volunteers' hard work and sacrifice weren't enough. Without trained teachers, textbooks, or supplies, many of the children fell behind. And those six hundred students were still only a small portion of the county's Black children.

What about everyone else? What would happen to them?

CHAPTER 7

SCRAMBLING

1959-1962

can easily tell anybody what happened with me," Ricky Brown said, recalling the school closings. "I played."[61] He wasn't the only one. Shirley Jackson said that "the first year the schools were closed, we played around with our friends."[62] Hundreds of other young children did the same thing. While their White neighbors were learning to read and write and do arithmetic, they played outside. At first, some children thought playing instead of going to school was fun. But after a week or two, most wished the schools would open. Some organized their dolls and pretended to be teachers. Others looked for anything they could find to read—old magazines and newspapers, catalogs, church hymnals, cereal boxes . . .

Older children like Douglas Vaughan had often worked part-time while they were in school. At twelve, Douglas was making money to help his older sister buy diapers and formula for her baby. When the schools closed, he started working longer hours at a veterinary hospital in Farmville.[63] Boys and girls who'd always done morning chores on their families' farms now spent most of the day doing farmwork.

Jerry Smith lived in a small house with a big family. He should have gone to fifth grade in 1959, but when the schools closed, he went to the training centers that volunteers had organized, and also spent a lot of time earning money mowing grass, painting—whatever he could do. He ran into some very good luck when he started delivering the *Richmond News Leader* newspaper every day. Jerry liked reading newspapers and read the paper before delivering it. He read other papers too, as many as he could get hold of. The *News Leader* had "a piece entitled 'A Point of Law,'" he remembered later. "It gave me insight on certain things and I read it every day. . . . Children started asking me things, as I seemed knowledgeable to them." He began to think of himself as "a little lawyer."[64] Reading the newspapers didn't make Jerry a lawyer, of course, but his reading and thinking skills improved even without a real school to go to. Most youngsters weren't that fortunate.

Some parents became their children's teachers. Sylvia Oliver watched the White children go by her window on their way to school and wanted to go to school herself. She and her sisters were lucky that their mother had been a substitute teacher and wasn't going to let the school closings stop Sylvia and the others from learning. Mrs. Oliver didn't allow her children to play all day. Sylvia recalled 1959 being "a rough year. . . . She [her mother] had the three of us at the kitchen table, not from sunup to sundown, but it was close."[65]

Carrie Clark was the second of five children and was ready to start fifth grade in 1959. Her mother had only gone to school through the fifth grade herself, but she and Carrie's father wanted their children to be educated. Mr. Clark sometimes worked for an older White woman who had been a teacher for many years. "She knew we wanted to learn," Carrie said, so she gave the family some textbooks to use. Despite her own lack of education, Mrs. Clark oversaw the children's schoolwork. Years later, Carrie described her mother's determination, saying, "She was crippled with rheumatoid arthritis, but she did not let that stop her classroom sessions. Mama made sure we read each day and did arithmetic from the book. All of us could read, write, and do math."[66]

Most families, though, had no way to get textbooks, and many mothers needed to go to work every day to earn money to buy food for their children.

School Closings in 2020

A coronavirus pandemic in 2020 forced schools to close suddenly and stay closed for months. In some ways, millions of families faced the same kind of problems Prince Edward County's families faced in 1959. Parents all over the country who had to go to workplaces every day scrambled to find supervision for their children. Some had to leave their children unsupervised for long periods of time. Parents who started working from home struggled to get their own work done while trying to oversee their children's schoolwork. Parents with little education themselves, or who didn't speak English well, couldn't help their children keep up. And low-income parents worried about their children missing school lunches.

However, there were enormous differences between the two situations. First and most important, the 2020 pandemic was a sudden, unintentional, natural disaster. The school closings in Prince Edward were planned, deliberate, and unnecessary. Second, school systems in 2020 worked quickly to put classes online and get materials to students. They didn't succeed everywhere, but they made huge efforts. Prince Edward's Black families had no school resources or materials at all, and county leaders did nothing to help them. Third, the 2020 pandemic kept most schools physically closed for about a year and a half, with children working online much of that time. The Prince Edward school closings lasted five years, with most children getting no education at all.

These mothers couldn't be their children's teachers at the same time. They hoped and prayed that the schools would open soon. The US Court of Appeals had agreed with the NAACP lawyers during the spring of 1959 and ordered the county to desegregate. Now, months later, the question was how long could the county get away with not funding any public schools at all?

Some White families faced similar problems when the schools closed. Even with tuition grants and vouchers, not every White family in Prince Edward could afford the Prince Edward Academy. A few refused to accept tuition

A crowd listens to a speaker at a rally organized by the NAACP on the steps of the Prince Edward County Courthouse, May 1961.

A young John Hines crouches in front of his siblings and parents for a family photo. John did not return to school after the seventh grade, when the public schools closed.

grants for the academy, either out of pride or because they believed in free public education. Without public schools and school attendance laws, the children of those families joined the county's Black children in losing out on an education.

John Hines, the son of a White farmer and logger, had finished seventh grade when the schools closed. John was used to working on the farm. He'd worked after school and during the summers for as long as he could remember. He'd even skipped school when his father needed him to work the tobacco. That was common among country children, and John liked working on the land and handling the farm equipment. He was happy when the schools stayed closed. But his younger siblings had barely started school.[67] What would happen to them if they stopped their education after first or second grade? Had county leaders thought about them?

As the weeks passed and the schools stayed closed, many Black parents scrambled to find solutions. Several Black teachers lived in Prince Edward and worked at Black schools in nearby counties. They took their own children and other Black children with them every day to attend those schools. Martha Morton taught elementary school in neighboring Charlotte County. When the Prince Edward schools closed, she started taking her daughter with her to the Charlotte school. She also piled four or five neighbor children into her Ford sedan (cars didn't have seat belts or child seats in the early 1960s).[68] The parents of children who lived in one county and attended school in another county were supposed to pay tuition since the family only paid taxes where they lived. But many principals looked the other way when it came to the Prince Edward County children. What was happening to them wasn't their fault or their parents' fault, and they needed to go to school. So the teachers kept loading their cars with as many children as would fit and kept their fingers crossed that the other schools wouldn't turn them away.

Families who could scrape together enough money rented houses in nearby counties so they could claim to be residents there. Dorothy Lockett's father worked for the railroad. Some of his White coworkers helped him rent a falling-down house in Appomattox County about twenty miles from his real home. The Locketts had no plans to live in the house. It wasn't even safe. But they worked to make it look like they lived there, fixing broken windows and putting up curtains, at least on the front. Every morning Mr. Lockett dropped his three children off on his way to work. "We stayed behind the house outside," Dorothy remembered. "When the bus arrived, we went in the back door, through the house, then out the front door and boarded the bus." Their older sister's three children went with them, all six youngsters packing into Mr. Lockett's car every morning. Word spread, and cousins and neighbors began arriving behind the old house each day. When they heard the noisy bus engine, they lined up to go through the house and out the front.

Eventually the Locketts did enough repairs on the house to make it livable and moved in. Children from other Prince Edward families continued to come every morning to meet the school bus. At one point, over twenty children came out the front door and got onto the bus.[69] The driver never asked how many children Mr. and Mrs. Lockett had.

Sylvia Oliver's family rented a house in Charlotte County after Sylvia and her sisters learned from books at the kitchen table that first year. The rented house wasn't nearly as nice as their own home, and the family included Sylvia's grandfather and great-grandfather. But she and her sisters were very happy to be going to school again, even though they'd had to trade running water and a bathroom in their real house for a well and an outhouse at the rental.[70]

Even years later, one memory from that time stuck with a lot of Black children: packing and unpacking. Some moved back and forth with their families or parts of their families, driving from their homes in Prince Edward to rented houses in neighboring counties. Others shuffled between their parents in Prince Edward and grandparents or aunts and uncles in other counties. They left home on Sunday night and returned on Friday, week after week after week.

Charlotte Herndon was just five years old when the schools closed. Her mother, a teacher in Prince Edward County, started teaching in a school over two hours away. She left Charlotte and her younger brother with their grandmother in Farmville and drove home to visit on weekends. The next year, Charlotte went with her mother to Spotsylvania so she could start first grade. "I did not think this was abnormal," she said later. "I didn't know we had schools in Prince Edward County." They followed the same pattern that other families did. "During Christmas, when school was out for about two weeks, we would open the house in Farmville . . . have the electricity and water turned on and the same in the summer."[71]

Other families turned to relatives, friends, and even strangers in nearby communities. At first, Lillian and Phyllis Jordan's father drove them a short distance to Appomattox County to get on a bus to the high school there every day. But so many Prince Edward children gathered at the same bus stop that Appomattox County authorities were bound to notice and tell them they couldn't attend the Appomattox schools. So Mr. Jordan made arrangements with a man he had met in a part of Charlotte County far from the Prince Edward line.

Early each morning, Lillian's mother drove the girls to Mr. Wilson's house, where they got on the school bus with the Wilson children to go to all-Black Central High School. Mrs. Jordan dropped the girls off, drove home, and then came back to pick them up in the afternoon. For Lillian and Phyllis, it meant traveling sixty miles a day plus the bus ride. It was twice that for their mother—one hundred twenty miles. She didn't hesitate to spend over three hours in the car every day if it meant her girls could go to school. Three hours added on to all the other things she did. Imagine what it meant to the family when Lillian and Phyllis graduated from high school on time.[72]

Some Black families sent children to live with relatives elsewhere. Shirley Jackson, who'd cried all the way home that day in 1959 when she'd learned her school was closed, eventually went with her sisters to live with another older sister, Mary Frances, about twenty-five miles from Farmville. Mary Frances and her husband, Franklin Gee, had three small children of their own, but they were willing to take the girls in so they could go to a real school. The Gee house was awfully full with eight people living there. They had no television and no phone either, and the girls missed talking to their mother. Mary Frances found herself cooking and caring for six children instead of three. She was willing, but the emotional and financial strain was hard on everyone.[73]

Angeles Wood hadn't yet started school when the county system shut down in 1959. At first, her older brothers played at home. But when the schools still hadn't opened two years later and Angeles turned six, her mother found ways to give all her school-aged children an education. Two of Angeles's older brothers went to live with a family friend in a nearby county. She and her sister Darlene went to family members in New Jersey. "Mama put a band around my wrist and one around Darlene's with important information," Angeles remembered. "She and Daddy put us on a Greyhound bus and we left Farmville." Think of it. Six years old and on a bus to go live in a strange place with aunts and uncles they hardly knew. "We started crying," Angeles said. Of course they did. What child wouldn't?

The girls had a cousin in Baltimore—John Stokes, the young man who had helped Barbara Johns plan the school strike ten years earlier. By 1961, he'd served two years in the army, finished college, and was teaching elementary school. Stokes met Angeles and Darlene at the bus terminal in Baltimore and took them home with him. Their uncle then drove down from New Jersey, put the girls into his car, and headed back to Jersey City, just across the Hudson River from Manhattan. Angeles and Darlene had traveled nearly four hundred miles to live and wouldn't even be together. Angeles was to stay with one aunt and uncle and Darlene with another, since neither family could afford to take care of both girls. They'd see each other on weekends. Over the next two years, they saw their parents and brothers and sisters just twice. Angeles never grew comfortable living in the big city. "Coming from the country, it was hard," she said. "People picked on you." And she missed her parents terribly. But that's what it took to go to school.[74]

The school closings hurt teachers as well as students. Prince Edward's seventy or so Black teachers lost their jobs. No matter how much they might have wanted to stay where they were, they needed paychecks and had to look elsewhere for teaching positions. Even if it meant separating their families.

Arnetta Winston had been teaching in Prince Edward

County for eight years. She was lucky enough to get a new teaching job in Halifax County, where she'd grown up. That meant she and her daughter lived in Halifax with her mother during the week and drove back home on the weekends to be with her husband, who worked in Farmville. It wasn't an easy way to be a family, but at least she had a teaching job.[75]

Dawes Orr and his wife Barbara Jamison Orr were both teachers in Prince Edward County. They, too, found new jobs, but Mrs. Orr's new position was in Charlottesville, Virginia, while Mr. Orr now taught in Maryland and visited his wife on weekends.[76] Other teachers were fortunate and went to work in neighboring counties close to home.

All over Prince Edward County, Black families faced the same hard decisions and made the same kinds of sacrifices. With each decision, parents who sent their children away wondered if they were doing the right thing. So did parents who kept their children at home. As the months passed, they all wondered if anyone outside Prince Edward County was paying attention. Why wasn't the state doing anything? Why wasn't the federal government doing anything? Why weren't the courts doing anything? The NAACP was still pressing its case, but it seemed never-ending. Didn't anyone anywhere outside the county care about what was happening in Prince Edward County?

CHAPTER 8

A NATIONAL SCANDAL

1960–1963

The Reverend Francis Griffin knew on the first day of the school closings that no government help was coming. The county government had destroyed its public schools. The state government had supported that destruction. And the federal government in Washington, DC. . . . well . . . the federal government had ignored Prince Edward County, as far as Griffin could tell. Reverend Griffin had tried to get President Eisenhower's attention in August 1959, just before the schools should have opened.

> *My Dear Mr. President,*
> *As Americans who believe in the authority and*
> *dignity of the law, we the members of the Prince*
> *Edward County Christian Association, appeal*
> *to you for whatever help you can offer in a tragic*
> *situation involving our county, state, and nation.*

Griffin reminded the president that segregation was immoral and illegal, and pointed out that the state and county had gone around the Supreme Court's ruling. He wrote that representative democracies needed educated citizens.

Griffin hoped Eisenhower would respond positively. Two years earlier, the president had sent federal troops to protect Black students entering Central High School in Little Rock, Arkansas. Surely, Griffin thought, he would do something for Black students in Virginia. But an assistant wrote back saying that the president "is powerless to take any action since public education is exclusively within the jurisdiction of the States."[77]

Griffin was very disappointed. But he didn't give up. Instead he worked harder than ever to find a way to help the children.

Most Americans had never heard of Prince Edward County, Virginia, even during the *Brown v. Board* hearings. But when news outlets reported on the school closings during the summer of 1959, the story found its way across the country. The national news magazine *U.S. News & World Report* wrote that "the nation is going to see, for the first time, what happens when an entire community abandons public schools and turns to private schools to escape integration."[78] The *Washington Post* said, "The stakes are high: A community's public schools and the education of its future citizens."[79] Civil rights and education activists watched carefully.

President Dwight D. Eisenhower talks to the nation about the situation at Central High School in Little Rock, Arkansas, September 24, 1957.

Jean Fairfax, an activist working for the American Friends Service Committee, a social justice organization founded by the Religious Society of Friends, or Quakers, knew someone had to do something in Prince Edward. Fairfax had worked with AFSC in Europe and Africa before deciding to focus on the Southern United States, where her grandparents had been born into slavery. She visited Prince Edward County soon after the schools closed.

Fairfax didn't plan to stay in the county herself. She had responsibilities all over the South. But she met with Reverend Griffin and others to discuss what AFSC could do to help the community. Then she asked Helen Estes Baker, another AFSC worker, to open an AFSC office in Farmville.

Baker had grown up in Virginia, attending all-Black schools near Norfolk. She'd been in education for more than thirty years and with the AFSC for ten years. Throughout that time, Baker had fought cancer—again and again. The constant struggle had taught her perseverance and hope. Six months before going to Prince Edward, she told a reporter, "I don't know anything more wasteful than fear."[80] That attitude would help her in her new position.

Baker arrived in Prince Edward County in October 1960 as the AFSC community relations director for the county. She quickly reached out to groups all over Virginia for their support, gathering supplies and donations for the training centers and setting up a teen center at the new AFSC office. True to her Quaker belief that every person has a divine inner light, she found ways of "taking the first awkward steps" toward better race relations. She brought together small groups of two Black women from Prince Edward and two White women from neighboring counties. She'd take the women for a driving tour of the area and to visit the training centers before having dinner with them. Many of these women, Black and White, had never had a real conversation with someone of a different racial background. She gave them an opportunity to find shared concerns and experiences.

Helen Baker also worked to develop community leadership. Prince Edward's Black community had suffered a real blow when the majority of Black teachers had left the county for jobs elsewhere. Those teachers had the respect of the whole community. They'd formed an important part of Prince Edward's Black middle class and were natural leaders. Everyone felt the loss of their skills and confidence. But Baker saw other people who could fill the gap. In particular, she admired the women who ran PECCA's training centers. They'd seen a need and stepped up to meet it. Baker started a leadership program to help them develop their talents. And she changed the lives of nearly seventy locked-out teens with the Emergency Placement Program.

The AFSC found host families around the country—people who could take in high school students from Prince Edward County for a year or more. Many of the families, but not all, were Quakers and familiar with the Friends' organization. Hosts lived in six different states, from Iowa to Massachusetts, and in small towns, big cities, and suburbs. The majority of volunteer hosts were Black families, but several White people and one Japanese American woman hosted as well. With Helen Baker's encouragement, dozens of Prince Edward students said goodbye to their families, got on buses, and went to live with strangers.

Imagine the challenges those students faced. Some had never been away from family or spent time in a big city. Most had never had a White teacher or classmates, or perhaps even spoken to a White adult. Imagine eating unfamiliar foods in an unfamiliar house where people spoke with unfamiliar accents and expressions. What if the students at the new school laughed at them? The local students were likely to be ahead academically since they hadn't missed a year or more of school. What if they were cliquish or bullies? What if the host family was mean? What if . . . ? This wasn't a couple of weeks away from home. It was a whole school year. And placement students felt like they had to show Black and White people in whatever city or state they went to that Black students from Prince Edward County were just as capable as anyone else. One young man said later that he'd never worked so hard at school in his life. "I couldn't fail. I wouldn't fail."[81]

Students who stayed with White families in White neighborhoods sometimes found themselves isolated at school. Neighbors could be unfriendly. But several White hosts reached out to local Black churches or neighbors to help the Prince Edward students feel more comfortable. One boy described being unhappy at first, but then getting to know White children and making friends. He thought adults had a harder time accepting him, but he said that the experience was "the greatest thing that ever happened to me."[82]

Barbara Bates went to a family in New Jersey and stayed for two years. She was only thirteen at the time, and she struggled with being away from home. Her hosts were a Black family and she socialized with their Black neighbors, but she was the only Black child in her class at school. "I never really felt that I belonged with the group in Moorestown. Most of the people there had lived there all their lives and I felt that I was intruding," she said, adding, "I'm not talking about the Whites now." Barbara was uncomfortable with her hosts and their friends. They weren't unkind or unfriendly. She simply felt like the outsider in a tight-knit community. She spoke differently, had grown up differently. And at thirteen it can be hard to feel a sense of belonging anywhere.

Barbara didn't give up on her education, though. She went to Massachusetts for her third year with the program and lived with a White family. Marveling at her host "father," she said later, "Mr. H. has three daughters. From the time I came there, though, he talked about his four girls." That could never have happened in Prince Edward County. Barbara made friends, and the experience changed her life for the better. But she felt sad when she realized that she would never choose to live in the South again.[83]

The American Friends Service Committee was the biggest effort to find host families for teens from Prince Edward, but it wasn't the only one. Another group recruited Black families in the Washington, DC, area to host students. Arthur Lee Foster went to live with the Swift family. They were Quakers, and Quaker Sunday services had no choir or pastor. That felt strange to Arthur, who'd grown up in the Baptist church. So the Swifts searched for a church that seemed more like home to him and drove him there every Sunday before going to their own meetinghouse. When he had trouble with his English classes at school, they found a woman who agreed to tutor him for free. The next year, he lived with his tutor and her husband, the Watsons. They encouraged him to go to college and even offered to help with the tuition.[84] He and the Watsons stayed in touch for years, and so did several other hosts and students.

Program leaders looked for host families, Black or White or Asian Americans, who would be good role models for the Prince Edward students. Many hosts were active in civil rights work. Many had overcome huge obstacles in their own lives. One Black host was a decorated veteran and part of the famous Tuskegee Airmen. A Black woman who hosted was a social worker and also a law student. At the time, very few women of any race went to law school. Host Victor Penzer, a Jewish immigrant to the United States, had been imprisoned in a Nazi concentration camp during World War II. As a Holocaust survivor, he knew the horror of prejudice and had wisdom to share.[85]

Prince Edward County teenager Moses Scott went to live with Penzer and his wife in Newton, Massachusetts. When he graduated from Newton High School there, he wrote a letter to the Newton community.

> We, the young students from Prince Edward attending school here[,] consider the opportunity to receive an education in a good school the greatest gift that we have ever received or ever shall receive.[86]

Scott spoke for a lot of placement students in Newton and elsewhere. But not every placement worked so well. The AFSC and other organizations were very careful in selecting host families. Even so, a small number of students found themselves with hosts who wanted them to act as maids or babysitters. Others didn't get along with their host families. And there were hosts who didn't understand the poverty some families in Prince Edward County's Black community faced. They were surprised when students didn't know how to use a flush toilet; they were unable to imagine that these young people actually had grown up with outhouses at home. They didn't understand why students didn't have more or better clothes. At the same time, most children in Prince Edward County had been taught to be quiet around strangers and couldn't imagine that their host families really expected them to have conversations with them.

In most cases, both families and students muddled through and got comfortable with each other over time. In the end, students made great progress at school and also learned a lot from getting to know new people, places, and ways of life.[87] They went home with a different view of the world and its possibilities.

Moses Scott called the opportunity for a good education a "gift." But that gift wasn't entirely free. Students and their families paid a hidden cost. Whether parents sent their young children to relatives in New Jersey or their teens to strangers in Massachusetts, those families were torn apart. Parents would never get over kissing their six-year-old goodbye and not seeing her again for months and months. Many Prince Edward homes had no phones, and in the days before cell phones and computers, living away from home meant no contact with family at all except for the occasional letter. No matter how caring a host family was, no matter how good it felt to go to school every day, the experience of being without mothers and fathers, sisters and brothers, took a toll on the children. It traumatized their parents, too.

Had the Prince Edward County Board of Supervisors thought about that trauma when they'd closed the schools? Had they assumed that all the county's Black parents would let their children go without education forever? Did they think that Black children who went away wouldn't miss their mothers as much as White children would if they went away? Think of the Black parents who had heard their grandparents' stories of being enslaved as young children. Stories of living with the knowledge that a White enslaver could break a family apart without a second thought. Now those parents saw their own families being separated. It wasn't forever, and it was a choice. But did it remind them of the stories they knew so well? Where did they find the courage to make that kind of sacrifice for their children's future?

Over time, other organizations from outside the county found ways to help at least some of Prince Edward's Black children. In July 1961, after the second year of closings, the

Virginia Teachers Association (a professional organization for Black educators) set up a summer program. Like PECCA's training centers, the program didn't try to replace regular schooling. The VTA leaders hoped to help children review what they had already learned and prepare to return to the classroom when the schools reopened, whenever that might be. The forty-seven volunteers from around Virginia and Washington, DC, stayed with families in the community. Some four hundred children came to review their skills and to feel like they were going to school. The AFSC's Jean Fairfax visited and commented that "these children were really hungry for education."[88] She was impressed by how much effort they put in all through the hot, steamy days of July. She saw how much they and their parents wanted the schools to reopen. How much they hoped that the NAACP lawyers' efforts in the courts and Reverend Griffin's nonstop work in the county and the state would succeed. But even with all the outside help and all the family efforts, the majority of the county's Black children had no schooling at all.

September came, and the chains and locks and NO TRES-PASSING signs on the public schools stayed where they were. There would be no school in 1961–62—a third year. Imagine the heartbreak.

VTA volunteers went back to their regular teaching

Students and a volunteer pose at a summer training, or "catch-up" program.

jobs. But they returned the next summer for another session of catch-up classes. A smaller group of mostly White college students from New England arrived as well. They worked closely with eight- and nine-year-old children who did not know how to read or write. Some of the children had never held a pencil or learned the alphabet. The volunteers did the best they could, but six or seven weeks over one summer couldn't make up for what those children had missed. Prince Edward's powerful White leaders had denied them the most critical years of their school lives.

In September 1962, disappointment fell over the Black community once more. The schools would not open in 1962–63—a *fourth* year without schools. Unbelievable.

Surely the courts would have to agree with the NAACP that denying a particular group of children an education violated the Fourteenth Amendment's guarantee that everyone must be treated equally under the law. But how many appeals would it take? How long would it be? What would happen to the children in the meantime?

Despite all the efforts, the numbers were grim. There were about 1,700 Black students (and about 1,500 White students) in the county in 1959. About 200 Black children should have entered first grade each year—in 1959, 1960, 1961, and 1962—but didn't. How many of those students were able to go to school outside the county?

There were

- 60 students who went to Kittrell Junior College,
- 70 who found student placements through AFSC,
- 25 who accepted placements in the Washington, DC, area,
- 100 who went to homes in other parts of Virginia through the VTA,
- an unknown number of families who moved out of the county permanently, with perhaps 50 children,
- another 100 who may have gone to family and friends,
- and many children who crossed county lines to other schools every day—maybe 600.

Do the math. About 1,000 students were able to keep going to school for some part of the time the schools were closed. That left at least 1,500 children—some 60 percent—with no formal education at all for as many as four years.

Fighting for a good cause can feel inspiring. Struggling alongside neighbors for that cause can give people a sense of real purpose, a sense that they are doing something that matters, something worth great sacrifice. But imagine going on day after day after day for *four years*. Four years of children growing up without the usual milestones—achievements like learning the alphabet or moving from one grade to the next. Events like graduations and award ceremonies. How could a child feel that her life was moving forward without those milestones? How could families celebrate for her? Black parents who had questioned their decisions when the schools had first closed questioned the choices they'd made again as time passed. Many believed firmly that "what we do in Prince Edward County, we do . . . for all disadvantaged and underprivileged people everywhere."[89] But as Reverend Griffin wrote later, "We suffered our children to be destroyed in order that the law might speak."[90]

CHAPTER 9

TURNING POINT

1963

D emocrat John F. Kennedy (JFK)—the youngest person and the first Catholic to be elected president of the United States—had taken office in January 1961. Kennedy hadn't been a strong supporter of civil rights as a member of the House or Senate. But the Democratic campaign *platform*, the outline of a political party's goals and positions on key issues, included a powerful statement on civil rights. One part of that statement pledged support for ending segregation in public schools.[91] During the campaign, Kennedy said, "I hope that the next president states that he stands for equal rights, that he stands for a fair chance for all Americans to have a decent education."[92] In the end, the election was extremely close, but JFK won with the help of some 70 percent of Black Americans' votes. Years later, one student who had been locked out of school said that Kennedy's election created a "dynamic change" among Black citizens in Prince Edward County.[93] They felt renewed energy and determination. But had the new president been sincere in what he'd said? Would he actually *do* anything?

Two weeks after his inauguration, President Kennedy spoke to reporters on several topics. In answer to a question about court orders to desegregate schools, he said,

> It is my position that all students should be given the opportunity to attend public schools regardless of their race, and that is in accordance with the Constitution. It is in accordance, in my opinion, with the judgment of the people of the United States. So there is no question about that.[94]

Kennedy still hadn't said he would take action. He hadn't promised to force Prince Edward County to open its schools, and probably didn't have the constitutional power to do so. Still, his openly supporting the *Brown v. Board of Education* decision gave the community hope.

President Kennedy appointed his brother Robert F. Kennedy (RFK) to be his attorney general, the head of the Department of Justice. The president got a lot of criticism for giving a relative such an important position in government, but Robert Kennedy took the job very seriously. RFK wanted to use the power of the federal government to help the NAACP in its lawsuit against Prince Edward County. However, the judge in the case had ruled in early 1961 that the Department of Justice could not join in—there was no law allowing it.

President John F. Kennedy signs an executive order
banning racial discrimination in housing that receives
federal assistance, November 1962. Kennedy faced
criticism for his weak support of civil rights legislation
before mid-1963.

RFK didn't give up. A few weeks later he spoke at the
University of Georgia. The atmosphere there was tense,
and several state leaders—all segregationists—refused to
attend because they were sure the attorney general would
discuss civil rights. They were right. Robert Kennedy

voiced his agreement with the 1954 decision in *Brown v. Board of Education*. "But," he said, "my belief does not matter—it is the law." Then he spoke of Prince Edward County. "I cannot believe that anyone can support a principle which prevents more than a thousand of our children in one county from attending public school. . . . We will not stand by. . . . We will move."[95]

How? When? What options did the federal government have? RFK wasn't specific. Finally, in March 1963, the attorney general talked once more about Prince Edward County, this time in a speech honoring the 1863 Emancipation Proclamation. He reminded his audience of the twentieth century's inequalities that harmed so many Americans.

> We must achieve equal education opportunities for all our children regardless of race. . . . We may observe with much sadness and irony that, outside of Africa, south of the Sahara, where education is still a difficult challenge, the only places on earth known not to provide free public education are Communist China, North Vietnam, Sarawak, Singapore, British Honduras— and Prince Edward County, Virginia.[96]

The school closings were an outrage. A disgrace. A national embarrassment.

During the 1960 presidential campaign, Reverend Griffin had written to both John Kennedy and his opponent, Republican Richard Nixon. "Will you use the powers of this great office to correct this evil . . . ?" he had asked the men then.[97] Now Griffin started pushing for federal government action again. He thought the time was right. "We had stayed out of the school long enough to let the world know that this was a nasty and unique situation," he said. "I thought that public sentiment [opinion] was sufficiently aroused."[98]

Griffin himself had helped to arouse that sentiment. He'd worked to keep Prince Edward County in the news. When Martin Luther King, Jr., had visited the county in the spring of 1962, King had called Griffin the county's "peerless leader," a leader without equal. King had encouraged Black residents there to vote—not easy in the South—and told them, "Do not despair, do not give up."[99] A few months later, Reverend Griffin appeared in an NBC News television special on the Prince Edward County schools. People all over the country watched. He said then that he worried about the morality of continuing the fight for desegregation and refusing to accept segregated schools while the court cases went on. He said he worried about the children who were suffering with no education at all. It was true. He did worry—he worried so much that stomach ulcers (open sores in the stomach) brought on by stress had forced him into the hospital for surgery to remove part of his stomach. But he told reporters and the country that he believed the "ultimate end is worth the sacrifice."[100]

White officials in Prince Edward stood firm against the negative publicity a visit from Martin Luther King, Jr., and a national news program gave them. And they generally ignored the AFSC and the volunteers who came to run the summer programs. They continued to say that the problem was the fault of the NAACP and Black leaders.

By this time, the Prince Edward Academy had a new, modern brick building on a large piece of land with plenty of space for sports fields and outdoor activities. There was a library with books on the shelves, and a woodworking shop along with enough classrooms for the high school students. Grades one through eight continued in church basements and the like while the foundation raised money to build an elementary and middle school.

Several White children who went to the academy said later that their education suffered during those early years. The lack of a real school building and equipment limited what and how they could learn. And the academy didn't have all the teachers it needed. One woman remembered that as a fourth grader she was taken out of her class to teach reading to a second-grade class. Think of that. A fourth grader *teaching* second grade because there weren't enough teachers. Other White men and women who'd been students at Prince Edward Academy admitted that they hadn't known at the time that local Black children had no school at all. It wasn't something they thought about since they'd never gone to school with their Black neighbors before the public schools closed. As children they hadn't understood what was happening, but their parents must have. How would those parents have explained it if the children had asked?

Imagine the frustration Black parents must have felt when they saw the new Prince Edward Academy under construction while their children fell further and further behind. That building was a lot like the Confederate Soldier Monument in Farmville—a symbol of White power.

Relations between White and Black county residents grew strained as time went on. A minister and journalist named Alfred Klausler visited the county from outside the state and wrote about "fear and tension among the residents." He described Prince Edward and the town of Farmville as places where "hatred smolders beneath the surface."[101] White people didn't talk about the school closings in public, and Black people didn't talk about the closings in front of their White neighbors. White women who hired Black housekeepers and maids simply didn't ask about their employees' children, even when they'd known each other for years. But everyone saw the reality as school buses picked up White children to go to the academy while Black children living on the same street watched from their yards.

Gordon Moss, the Longwood professor who spoke out against the school closings, believed that a handful of five or six White men controlled the entire situation—men including J. Barrye Wall and other unelected leaders. Moss was sure that without them, the rest of the White population would not have closed the public schools. But most county officials, business owners, and others would never speak out or stand up for reopening the schools as long as those few men were in control. Their intimidation, their bullying of the White community, had been effective.

Reverend Griffin refused to be afraid and refused to give up. He was certain there must be something the federal government, the Kennedy administration, could do. In early 1963, Griffin met with Justice Department officials in Washington to discuss possible solutions. Government experts argued that the federal government could not legally open and run schools in Virginia. The Constitution didn't allow it. The federal government could not provide the money for schools either. But the government *could* share its know-how in setting up schools if the school was funded with private donations. And it could suggest ways to get those private donations. Griffin was ready.

In May, Robert Kennedy hired an assistant, a young

lawyer with experience helping people in crisis. William vanden Heuvel listened as Kennedy described the situation in Prince Edward County and the president's concern for the children there. Both the attorney general and the president wanted schools up and running in Prince Edward County in September 1963. Could vanden Heuvel do it? Could he pull together a plan for those schools in just three months? Vanden Heuvel went to work, driving to and from Farmville more times than he cared to count.

Finally. Finally, the future looked brighter than it had for a very long time. The Free Schools, as they were called, weren't a permanent solution. But surely the courts would force the county to open the public schools soon. Appeals were moving through the system.

The Appeals Process

If one side of a criminal or civil court case believes that the court's decision is unjust or that there was something wrong with the trial or the law, that side may appeal the verdict. This means that they may ask a higher court—an appeals court—to review the decision and perhaps overturn it. An appeal is not a new trial. The appeals court looks at whether the original trial followed the law and was fair. Appeals courts usually have more than one judge hearing each appeal. Most states have three levels of courts—trial courts, appeals courts, and the state supreme court, which is the highest level of appeal in the state.

The federal court system also has three levels— federal district courts, where trials are held; US courts of appeals (also called "circuit courts"); and the United States Supreme Court. The US Supreme Court is the nation's highest court of appeals for both federal and state court decisions. The nine justices of the US Supreme Court may hear appeals and over-turn decisions from lower federal courts and from state supreme courts. A lawsuit can go from a state court to a state appeals court to a state supreme court and then to the US Supreme Court before the decision is absolutely final.

In the meantime, the Free Schools would offer free education to any child in Prince Edward County, Black children and White children alike. If done well, the plan would be a model for educating children in disadvantaged areas across the country. Change was coming. Moreover, the promise of schools wasn't the only shift taking place in Prince Edward County.

While administrators raced to set up schools for 1,500 children in just weeks, and volunteer teachers and college students offered summer programs again, civil rights activists organized too. Twelve years earlier, when students at Moton High School had gone on strike, the modern civil rights movement had been just beginning. Now, in 1963, that movement was alive and active throughout the United States. Prince Edward County was no exception. Black voices there demanded more than integrated schools.

J. Samuel Williams was a junior at R. R. Moton High School when Barbara Johns organized the 1951 strike. He took part in the strike that April and then became senior class president when school opened in September. Williams remembered later how awful the conditions at Moton High School had been. But he also remembered the positive impact the teachers there had had on him. In particular, he talked about one teacher who spent part of every day teaching Black history.

At the time, American history textbooks rarely mentioned Black Americans, Asian Americans, or women of any race—almost no one other than White men. Williams and his classmates thought at first that their teacher was making up stories. They didn't know that Black people in the United States had done important things. Learning about Harriet Tubman and Marcus Garvey and others was eye-opening. Students at the White high school would never learn about these men and women. And when the same teacher announced that he didn't care what the school superintendent—a White man—said, Sam Williams reported that it "opened a new door in my mind." He'd had no idea that a Black man could stand up to a White man.[102]

Williams joined the army after graduation and eventually went to Shaw University in North Carolina, the same school that Reverend Griffin had attended. Like Griffin, Williams had decided to become a minister. At Shaw, he got involved in sit-in demonstrations where young Black college students went to segregated lunch counters, sat down, and asked to be served. Some demonstrators faced arrest for violating Jim Crow laws. Some sat calmly while angry White customers poured ketchup or syrup or coffee on them. In several places, White businesses closed rather than giving in to serving Black customers. Sam Williams came away from those protests with a good understanding of nonviolent demonstrations and new organizing skills.

On weekends, Williams often drove back to Farmville to help Reverend Griffin at the church. He also took on the work of encouraging Black adults in Prince Edward County to register to vote. At first, he didn't think he'd have much success. After all, White supremacists had kept Black citizens from voting for decades. But it turned out that many people in the Black community were ready to get past the old intimidation. "I discovered there was more determination among the people than I thought," he said. "I began to see things in a different light."[103] Even so, only about 25 percent of Prince Edward's Black residents registered to vote in the early 1960s, compared to 50 percent of White residents in the county.[104] But that was more than in previous years.

During the spring of 1963, Williams began planning demonstrations in downtown Farmville. A few of the new activists were the younger brothers, sisters, and cousins of the Moton strikers. They respected Williams for his role all those years ago. By late July, they and other Black high school and college students were getting instructions from members of the nationally known Student Nonviolent Coordinating Committee (SNCC, pronounced "snick").

Betty Jean Ward's parents had sent her to live with her grandparents and go to school in the next county while her older brother Ronnie and sister Phyllistine went to Kittrell Junior College to finish high school. When the college students from SNCC arrived in Farmville, Betty Jean was home for the summer and eager to learn from them. "SNCC took us to the property of Barbara Johns's father and trained us," she said. "SNCC taught us how to protect ourselves. We went through drills. If water was sprayed on us, we were taught what to do. If the dogs were put on you, we were taught how to respond."[105]

Imagine preparing to be hit with the powerful stream from a fire hose or attacked by a police dog. Imagine preparing for that willingly. Dozens of young people took part. On weekends, they carried signs with slogans such as WE AREN'T DROPOUTS, WE ARE LOCKOUTS and FREE EDUCATION IS OUR INALIENABLE RIGHT. Other signs demanded that businesses hire Black employees at the same pay that White workers got. Like protesters in other places, they faced arrest and White anger.

"We had the town squirming," Betty Jean said. "The buzz . . . was that the Black folk were trying to take over."

That buzz led to retaliation. Betty Jean described the threats that parents of young demonstrators faced. "The manager at Taylor Manufacturing Company told workers: 'If you don't get your children off the streets, you are going to lose your job.'"[106] That manager wasn't alone.

Brenda Smith picketed the business where her grandfather worked. White police officers arrested her along with several other young people. But she wasn't afraid, or didn't let anyone know that she was afraid. Even when a fellow protestor saw people drop lit cigarettes into the hair of Black demonstrators, Brenda and the others refused to be intimidated. When they went to court after their arrest, "The judge asked each of us if we knew what we were doing. The answer was yes, I want the same freedom that everyone else has in Farmville."[107]

During the summer of 1963, young Black people protested discrimination in Farmville, Virginia.

During July and August 1963, Black county residents—many of them teens who had gone north in the student placement program—spent hours on the streets of Farmville. One group would picket for two or three hours in Virginia's thick summer heat and then go back to a Black church to rest while another group took their place.[108]

They made some progress. Three store owners agreed to hire Black workers rather than lose Black customers, and a department store allowed Black shoppers to try on clothing. But teens and college students weren't the ones spending money in Farmville, and it wasn't easy to convince older Black people in a place like Prince Edward County to boycott (stay away from) businesses.

Sandy Stokes, Everett Berryman, and Emerson Hunt protest in Farmville, 1963.

If residents didn't shop in Farmville, they had to go fifty miles to buy groceries or anything else. Working people couldn't afford the time or the gas for that.

The protests had a bigger effect on the young people who participated in them. The training and the demonstrations gave them a sense of their own power. It might take a long time, but they believed they could move Prince Edward County in the right direction. Black activists all over the United States felt the same way.

In late August, Prince Edward's Black residents, young people and older, had an opportunity to show their determination in front of the nation and the world. Reverend Griffin reserved eighty-two seats on charter buses so that the county would be represented at the March on Washington for Jobs and Freedom, scheduled for August 28. For months, major civil rights organizations had been planning the march and demonstration to demand federal civil rights legislation. They wanted an end to Jim Crow laws, an end to the delays in desegregating schools, and protection of the right to vote, as well as a new government focus on jobs for the unemployed. As the date approached, more and more organizations announced their support, including both Black and White religious groups and labor unions. Black and White entertainers signed on to participate too—theater, film, and television stars Sammy Davis, Jr., and Lena Horne; folk singers Bob Dylan and Peter, Paul and Mary; and world-renowned gospel singer Mahalia Jackson.

About eighty Prince Edward County residents joined the March on Washington for Jobs and Freedom in August 1963.

Several of the Prince Edward County residents who went to Washington that day had never been far outside the county. The biggest town they'd ever seen was Farmville, with a population of just over 4,000. They boarded the buses for the four-hour ride to the nation's capital and gathered to march with over 250,000 men, women, and children—masses of Black marchers with tens of thousands of White marchers among them. The Prince Edward demonstrators walked together, carrying a huge banner in front of them. It said simply: PRINCE EDWARD. That's all it needed to say. Everyone everywhere now knew about Prince Edward County.

The March on Washington on August 28, 1963, drew some 250,000 people from across the country to the nation's capital. No gathering on the National Mall and no civil rights demonstration had ever attracted so many people before.

There had never been an event like this. Marchers moved shoulder to shoulder past the famous monuments and memorials, the Capitol and the White House. They held hands and sang—packed together on the National Mall in front of the Lincoln Memorial. No gathering in Washington, DC's history had ever attracted so many people. Before the hot, glorious day was over, Martin Luther King, Jr., gave the most famous speech of his life—"I Have a Dream."

Try to imagine what being in that crowd must have felt like. Think of the energy that ran through such an enormous group of people all sharing the same goal and the same determination. Picture the mood on the buses as the Prince Edward County group rode home that night. Like Dr. King, Prince Edward's Black community had a dream. A big part of that dream was good schools. They'd made enormous sacrifices for that dream for twelve years now. Perhaps they could finally realize their dream *if* the Free Schools opened in September.

CHAPTER 10

THE FREE SCHOOLS

1963

G etting the Prince Edward County Free Schools off the ground was a whopper of an assignment on short notice. Especially with the whole country watching. Fortunately, William vanden Heuvel was young and optimistic. He was also very competent. Only in his early thirties, he was an attorney and had been an assistant to the governor of New York and to a US ambassador. He had also worked with the International Rescue Committee, helping refugees in war-torn parts of the world.[109]

Now he spent July and August going back and forth between his office in Washington and a temporary office in Farmville, with side trips to Richmond. He needed support from Virginia state officials and from Prince Edward County officials, the very men who had closed the schools in the first place. He needed support from Virginia state officials and from Prince Edward County officials, the very men who had closed the schools in the first place. He needed the trust and support of the NAACP and the county's Black community. Would they believe a White

William vanden Heuvel, an assistant to Attorney General Robert Kennedy, took the lead in creating free schools for Black students in Prince Edward County in 1963.

government official from Washington after hearing false promises for decades? And there was the money. The schools would cost at least a million dollars (nearly nine million dollars today) for one year, and it had to come from private donations—foundations, corporations, individuals. . . .

Vanden Heuvel managed to arrange a meeting with the governor's staff, representatives from the NAACP, and Prince Edward County's White leaders. After hours of negotiations, they worked out an agreement on the Free Schools. The federal government would take the lead in organizing. The governor of Virginia would appoint an interracial board of trustees to oversee the schools. And the county officials would agree to lease public school buildings to the Free Schools. Money started to trickle in after President Kennedy made a personal donation of $10,000 and then contacted the heads of charitable foundations and wealthy friends, asking them to donate. It's not easy to say no to a personal request from the president of the United States.

It made sense that not everyone in Prince Edward County trusted the Free Schools agreement. Some summer volunteer teachers called it a "hoax." They were sure that powerful Virginians didn't want the Free Schools to succeed. Reverend Griffin, however, supported the plan. The county was on edge, and the Free Schools could be a temporary fix.[110]

Griffin had spent the summer with the protesters in Farmville. He loved the young people's determination and spirit, even as he reminded them to maintain non-violence no matter what. But he worried. In early June, White police and temporary deputies in Danville, Virginia, some ninety miles south of Farmville, had used fire hoses against a prayer vigil and injured dozens of peaceful Black participants. The cracks that had always existed in the shell of the Virginia way were growing bigger and deeper as more and more Black citizens stepped "out of line" to demand their constitutional rights. Now the local Prince Edward police department of four officers had hired fifty temporary deputies.[111] Did the police chief expect terrible trouble? Or were those deputies there to intimidate Black demonstrators? Would they attack peaceful protestors as the deputies in Danville had? William vanden Heuvel said, "The community was . . . boiling. . . . Some people are even predicting bloodshed if the schools aren't reopened."[112] Griffin wondered how much longer he or anyone else could keep things calm. The Free Schools had to open. And they had to succeed.

Vanden Heuvel felt terrible pressure to find good people to run the schools and was relieved in the last week of August when he interviewed Neil Sullivan for the job of superintendent. Sullivan had never lived in the South. He'd never overseen a school filled with children who'd been denied an education. He was from New England and was now the superintendent of schools in a small, fairly wealthy district in Long Island, New York. New York didn't have segregation laws, but no Black families lived in Sullivan's school district, so all of the schools' students were White. Why did vanden Heuvel want to hire him?

Neil Sullivan believed in integration and had hired Black teachers to teach White children. He also had a reputation for bringing new ideas into education. He'd introduced *nongraded* schools in his district. Students in a nongraded school worked at their own pace and could move to the next grade level in one subject before moving ahead in another subject. They could advance before or after their classmates did. That sounded like what Prince Edward County students needed. No one knew how many children had been learning at home and how many hadn't. School officials and teachers needed to be ready to help children of all ages learn to read for the first time.

Sullivan didn't accept the job immediately. He wanted to visit Prince Edward County first. He saw the young protesters on Main Street. He saw bearded college students from New York sitting on the courthouse steps, giving a lesson to local children. He drove past beautiful Southern homes in town, along with a Whites-only swimming pool and a Whites-only, lighted baseball field. Some sections of town had Black and White families living quite near each other, but the neighborhood across the railroad tracks where he saw only Black people was terribly poor and run-down. Some houses even had outhouses in their backyards right there in town. In the countryside, the sight of young, too-thin children cutting enormous tobacco leaves in the blistering heat shocked him.[113] He'd never seen that kind of poverty.

Sullivan spent hours talking with Black families and White families. He was convinced that his ideas, especially his ideas about nongraded classes, could work very well in Prince Edward County. They could meet the needs of the children there. But he also talked with J. Barrye Wall, publisher of the *Farmville Herald* and a leader of the Defenders. He listened to the man's reasons for opposing the Free Schools. Wall was polite and didn't show any anger or hostility. But Sullivan knew that he and the *Farmville Herald* publisher wouldn't agree on much of anything. That was too bad since Wall's newspaper was the biggest voice in the White community.

Next, Sullivan met with Reverend Francis Griffin and realized right away that he'd found someone he could rely on. An ally for the Free Schools. Only a few families had asked to enroll their children in the schools, and it was already the last week of August. But Griffin oozed confidence. "I predict that the Free School Association will have the full support of Prince Edward County Negroes," he said. "It most assuredly will have mine."[114]

Neil Sullivan also spent time with Gordon Moss from Longwood College. Moss, a White teacher at a White college, had spoken out against the school closings from the start. But he hadn't been a supporter of desegregation at the time.

Gordon Moss had grown up surrounded by segregation, just as Harry Byrd, J. Barrye Wall, and the rest of the White power structure had. Moss, however, was willing to question his own thinking and let facts and evidence lead him toward new ideas. And he thought seriously about his Christian beliefs and what they meant. He said later that "when the schools closed, I knew I couldn't live with myself unless I fought it."[115]

As the school stalemate had dragged on and Moss had made his voice louder, he'd started working with Reverend Griffin, Jean Fairfax of the AFSC, and other Black leaders. He saw that he'd been wrong in his beliefs on race. He admitted that it had taken him sixty years, but in the end he went from being a supporter of public schools for all, but segregated public schools, to arguing for true equality and integration.

Gordon Moss had been a very popular history professor at Longwood since 1944 and had been appointed as a dean (somewhat like a principal) in 1960. He was generous with his time at the college and in the community, meeting with students and volunteering as treasurer of his church in

Farmville. His wife had been ill and in and out of hospitals for years, which left most of the raising of their three still-young children to him. It was a lot to deal with, but Moss came across to Neil Sullivan as happy and positive.

Sullivan described the man with white hair, dark eyebrows, and a bow tie as "one of the kindest, most gentlemanly individuals" he'd ever met. Yet by 1963 when the two men met, Gordon Moss had plenty of reason to be angry or resentful.[116] Despite all the good he did in town and at Longwood, speaking out against the Defenders of State Sovereignty and Individual Liberties early on had cost Moss friends and respect. As his views shifted and he began to call for real equality, things only got worse.

One White county resident wrote in a letter that appeared in the *Farmville Herald*, "Why doesn't Dr. Moss resign his position at Longwood or get a job in a place more to his liking, where he can spend all his time integrating the races?"[117] Two or three other professors who agreed with Moss had left Longwood and gone elsewhere to work just as high school principal Bash and Reverend Kennedy had. Moss ignored the critics and stayed in Farmville. He had said in 1962, "I am not the only White person in Prince Edward County who is violently opposed to what is going on. . . . I am simply the most garrulous [talkative]."[118] But was he right? Were there others?

Two years earlier, in 1960, a group of White businessmen had met very quietly to discuss ways to reopen the public schools. When they left their meeting, they found a number of Defenders and members of the Prince Edward School Foundation, waiting. By the next day, papers appeared all over Farmville and the county listing the names of the men who had met, calling them "traitors," and claiming that they would "sell their honor and the moral upbringing of our white children for a few dollars." Store owners who'd been to the meeting lost customers. Others lost their jobs.

The group soon dissolved and its members went silent. By the time Gordon Moss claimed to be the most talkative White person to oppose the closings, he was very nearly the *only* White person who would say anything at all.[119] And he continued to pay for it.

Local White citizens sent petitions to Longwood demanding that Moss be fired. He wasn't. He kept his teaching job, but was assigned only freshman-level world history classes. That wasn't his field of expertise, and he considered the assignment an insult.[120] But he didn't back down. And he didn't back down when his position angered his church.

During a "kneel-in" in Farmville in August 1963, young Black activists attempted to enter White churches for Sunday services. Most of those churches turned them away, and more than twenty peaceful Black protesters were

Dr. Gordon Moss on his front porch across the street from Longwood College. Moss refused to give in to White supremacists' pressure.

arrested. Ushers at the Episcopal church that Gordon Moss belonged to allowed a small group of Black young people to enter, but members of the congregation were shocked when Moss approached the group and invited the young people to sit with him. He lost his position as church treasurer the next day.

Professor Moss could have found another college teaching job somewhere else. He could have joined another Episcopal parish. But he chose to stay where he was and keep speaking out against White supremacy. Neil Sullivan wondered about that. Moss explained,

> I've been teaching American history for forty years. I've been teaching that democracy and social justice are the greatest ideals of the American nation. I'd be a traitor to the thousands of students I've taught if I didn't take a stand for these ideals when the opportunity comes.[121]

As Sullivan got ready to leave Farmville, he thought about what he'd seen and heard, the people he'd met, and the sacrifices they'd made. On the way out of town, he talked to a young protester whose parents had been able to send her to live with friends and go to school in a nearby county. She considered herself "privileged." But, she said, "I want my little brothers and sisters to go to school too, because they've been at home all these four years." She'd heard about the Free Schools. "They would really be my salvation. They would just be salvation for my whole family."[122]

Neil Sullivan decided to accept the job as superintendent of the Free Schools.

The Prince Edward Free Schools were scheduled to open on September 16, just two and a half weeks after Neil Sullivan became superintendent. They would use four school buildings rented from the county. But as hard as William vanden Heuvel and a number of men and women in Prince Edward had been working all summer, only a superintendent could hire staff for the four buildings, buy supplies, and more.

The new Moton High School, built after the student strike, was very nice except for four years of dust. It would become the high school for the Free Schools. But the building had almost no equipment. Some people suspected that staff and parents of students at the Prince Edward Academy had taken everything. The other three buildings also lacked equipment, and they needed massive repair work—everything from fixing leaking roofs, cracked plaster, and rotting floorboards, to cleaning the horrid filth and stench from open urinals and garbage left behind four years earlier. Some twenty school buses sitting abandoned for four years all needed new tires and batteries, oil, and someone to drive them.[123]

Then there were books to order—textbooks for every subject at every grade level for some 1,500 students.

The schools needed cafeteria equipment and cafeteria workers, principals for the four schools, custodians, lab supplies, art supplies, pencils, paper, copy machines, and—most important of all—teachers. One hundred teachers. Reverend Griffin had been right about people supporting the Free Schools. Student registrations were pouring in.

Advertisements for teachers went out to every college and university in the country that had an education program, every large school district and teachers' organization, the military, church organizations, and news outlets. But school systems everywhere needed qualified teachers. There simply weren't enough, and teaching at the Free Schools would be difficult and temporary.

At the end of his first week on the job, Neil Sullivan felt nearly hopeless.

> I had worked feverishly all week and had recruited fourteen teachers. I did not have a single bus driver and I needed twenty. I had more children registering than I had available classrooms. I had received an ever-increasing number of crank letters. And I was terribly tired.[124]

Sullivan went back to the hotel where he was staying. He hadn't been able to find anyone willing to rent him a house. Some White landlords had rejected him because he might entertain Black people in his home. Others had rejected him because he was a Catholic (anti-Catholic prejudice was common in the South at the time). He went to bed exhausted, but at two o'clock in the morning, the phone rang. A man's voice said, "Go on home, you n_____ lover!" The new superintendent had to wonder what he'd gotten himself into.[125]

Fortunately, the next week was better. Much better, as skilled workers, office assistants, and volunteers pulled the schools together. Building repairs moved along, families stood in line to register students, and applications from well-qualified teachers arrived. A few days before the scheduled opening, Sullivan held a faculty meeting. He started by leading everyone in the Pledge of Allegiance. When they finished, no one spoke. Finally a retired teacher who'd chosen to come to Prince Edward for one year to help the children said, "I've been repeating that oath all my life and only now, at seventy, do I really understand what it means."[126] Think about that.

About half of the Free Schools' teachers were from Virginia, and a handful of those Virginians were White. White teachers teaching Black students was practically unheard of in the state. The other half of the staff came from all over the country. Altogether, about 30 percent of the faculty was White, 70 percent Black. Sullivan told them,

Almost half of our total school enrollment will be entering a classroom for the first time in their lives. A great many will be unable to read. You'll find nine- and ten-year-olds who never heard of the alphabet. . . .

No one can give back to these children the four years of schooling they have missed, but our great task will be to help each youngster make up as much lost time as he possibly can as quickly as he possibly can.[127]

The teachers were willing to take that on. But there was another concern. The Prince Edward Free Schools were open to all of the county's children, Black and White. Yet while Sullivan was very pleased to have an integrated faculty, no White students had registered. If there were no White students at all, the Free Schools would not have met their goal.

Gordon Moss's oldest child, a boy, had been ready to start high school when the county had closed the public schools. Moss wouldn't send his son to the Prince Edward Academy and instead sent him to a school in Lynchburg, about fifty miles west. Now Richard (Dickie) Moss was about to enter his senior year, not a time when most students want to transfer to a new school. He knew his neighborhood friends might turn on him the way his father's friends had if he went to the Free Schools. But the young Moss had watched his father's courage for four years. As he described it later, "It was something I could do for my dad. He'd been fighting this battle for a long time." After a lengthy conversation with his parents, Richard Moss decided to enroll in the Free Schools, even if he would be the only White student there.[128]

Not long after, another White student enrolled. Letitia Tew was eight years old and had not yet started school. Her parents believed in free, public education and would not send her to the academy. Superintendent Sullivan pointed out that the little girl might be the only White child in the elementary school. "I wouldn't be troubled by that," her mother answered. "We believe school should be free. . . . Right is right."[129]

With just two days to go, reporters from television networks and major newspapers and magazines crowded into nearby hotels. The Free Schools were a national story. Teachers decorated their classrooms with posters and bulletin boards—*after* they'd washed windows and floors and hauled equipment around. Even some reporters pitched in to help. Bus drivers practiced their routes and reminded the children they saw that school would start on Monday.

On Sunday afternoon, Neil Sullivan enrolled two more

White students after their father asked him to come to their house. The family was new in the county and had a small tobacco farm. Mr. Abernathy feared bringing his children to town to register for the Free Schools. He didn't want to talk to reporters or, worse, meet hostile White residents. Virginia's shell of good manners had cracked even further. White people like Moss and Tew and Abernathy made segregationist residents angry. They were traitors to the sacred cause of White supremacy. The Tew family had received threats, even against the bus that Letitia would ride to school. And someone told Letitia's mother she should have her head chopped off if she sent her daughter to the Free Schools.[130] In the end, Mr. Abernathy listened to all the concerns and decided to send his children to the Free Schools despite his fear. He wanted them to have the education he'd never gotten, and they were eager to get started.

Sullivan felt good as he reached his hotel late that Sunday afternoon. Four White students wasn't a lot, but it did mean that the Free Schools were desegregated—as desegregated as a lot of other public schools in Virginia. Perhaps more White students would register in the next few days. And a big truckload of supplies had arrived as well. He and his team would meet their deadline.

He entered his hotel more confident than he'd been all week. But the chill of a sudden, heavy silence hit him the instant he walked into the hotel lobby. News had just come across the radio and television. Someone had thrown a bomb into a Sunday school at a Black church in Birmingham, Alabama. Four young girls were dead, and more than a dozen other children were hurt, some of them terribly injured. Who would attack a children's Sunday school? What could spur that kind of hatred? The Birmingham public schools had obeyed a court order and desegregated days earlier. That had angered White supremacists. The bombing was their response.

Americans all over the country that Sunday night saw the horrifying pictures on television. They saw the gaping hole the dynamite had made and the rubble that had filled it and had blasted across the sidewalk and into the street. They saw a shattered stained-glass window and the many empty window frames where stained glass had been. They saw the numb shock on the faces of the people standing across the street as they watched investigators in stunned silence.

How would the Prince Edward Free Schools open in the morning? Would parents be afraid to send their children to school? Would teachers be afraid for their lives?

CHAPTER 11

UP AND RUNNING

1963–1964

T here was no choice. Everyone had to shake off the horror of what had happened in Birmingham and focus on a successful opening for the children in Prince Edward the next morning. Or they had to at least pretend they'd shaken off the horror. Teachers shouldn't have to be courageous as well as educated and skilled and caring to do their jobs. But the Free Schools teachers dug deep to put their fear aside and go to their schools early on Monday. They greeted their new students even as they looked and listened for signs of trouble. No matter what they were feeling, they smiled and kept smiling.

Students had their own worries, both those who knew about the bombing in Birmingham and those who might not have heard the news. Some children were eager to start school; some were scared. Many were both. Hundreds of young and older children gathered outside the four school buildings with the unmistakable jitters of the first day of school. At nine o'clock, the school bells started ringing. And ringing. At one school, the bell rang for a full thirty seconds. A custodian explained that he'd planned to "lean on this bell and lean on it hard. It's been too long not ringing."[131]

Children enter Mary E. Branch school, part of the Free Schools, September 16, 1963.

Anthony Farley was fourteen in September 1963. He said later,

> When the Free School opened, that was one of the most exciting days of my life. It was like Easter Sunday. Everybody had their best clothes on. Your mama went out and bought the boys Converse sneakers. The girls had on pretty white and pink dresses.[132]

Anthony should have started fifth grade in 1959. He'd stayed home for the next four years but had gone to the training centers and summer programs. He felt ready for school. During the earliest days, all the students took tests to see where they were in their education. Most of those who'd gone to school in other counties or states while the schools had been closed did well. They were right where they should be. Those who hadn't gone to actual schools all that time were another story. Anthony remembered,

> After the testing, some students were fourteen and in the third grade. Can you imagine being fourteen years old and in the third grade with your cousin who was eight years old?

He was fortunate. He tested at the eighth-grade level, just one year behind where he should have been, so he didn't feel out of place.[133] One of his classmates was sixteen and had a harder time adjusting.

Travis Harris had spent four years going to church-sponsored night classes when he could, and working during the day for nearby White farmers. Big for his age, and strong, he said later, "I was hired as a boy but worked like a man." That made school rules and routines difficult for him. "I felt awkward," he said. "I had been in the company of grown men. . . . I was not used to holding my hand up in the air and asking for a hall pass to go to the bathroom."

Soon after he started his classes, Travis wanted to quit. He needed help in some subjects where he was only at a sixth-grade level. That meant staying after school and working with tutors during study halls. It was hard and embarrassing. But his parents insisted he stay in school. "Even the White people I worked for said, 'Stay in school because you do not want to farm all your life.'"[134] He stayed, but other students like him had an even worse time.

John Hurt had been ready to start second grade when the county had closed the schools. He'd gone to bed every night for weeks feeling sure school would start the next day. But it didn't. Like the majority of Black children in Prince Edward, he and his brothers and sisters had no schooling at all for the next four years, not even at the training centers or summer programs. When the Free Schools opened, it seemed like a dream come true. But John soon felt the impact of that lost time. Years later, he explained, "I was put in sixth grade . . . and had never completed the second grade. I was reading 'See Jane run.' I was bigger than any of the children in my class. It was so embarrassing. . . . It was just too late."[135] John Hurt wasn't alone. One student recalled "sixteen-, seventeen-, eighteen-year-old kids, in classrooms with nine- and ten-year-olds; and somehow you know that formula is not going to work out."[136] How would a young adult manage in a class with nine-year-olds? Think of the awkwardness, the fear of looking stupid or ignorant.

Younger children faced different challenges. Many wanted to go to school as much as Anthony Farley did, but they weren't prepared. They had almost no experience with people outside their families and closest neighbors, and no experience in a school setting. Some of those children were terribly shy and quiet. They wouldn't make eye contact with adults and hesitated to speak at all, even turning their faces to the wall when teachers walked by. Children who should have been in third or fourth grade didn't know how to hold a pencil. A lot of students had never owned a book. How could that be? In some cases, their parents had never learned to read. Most poor families couldn't afford to buy books, and the county library was Whites-only. When a Free Schools librarian offered one boy of ten or eleven a book, he wouldn't take it. He ran out of the room saying, "I can't read." A girl started crying when she realized she needed to learn from "babyish" books.[137]

Teachers and administrators saw right away that they had to adjust their plans to reach these children who had missed out on so much. The school staff came early and stayed late. They often met together in the evenings to

Free School students and teachers, 1963.

share their successes and get ideas from each other. All the faculty agreed that the Free School students were eager to learn. They needed teachers who were ready to do everything possible to help them succeed.

Before long, most of the children lost their shyness and started acting more like children in other schools—playing, laughing, making noise. They opened up, even smiling and volunteering answers in class. An editorial in the *New York Times* said that "a measure of relief has finally been arranged for one of the most shocking acts of deprivation ever inflicted on the Negro."[138]

While national newspapers and news programs

reported on the Free Schools. However, most White county residents seemed to ignore them. It was as if they hadn't seen all the preparation, all the school buses, all the children. As if they hadn't noticed reporters and government people around town. The few people who did take note let it be known that they didn't like what they saw.

Superintendent Sullivan and his wife, a reading specialist who was teaching at the elementary school, had finally rented a house near Farmville. But car horns often blared outside their windows in the middle of the night. They got up on many mornings to find garbage in their front yard. And they didn't often see the courtesy and pleasant manners that earlier visitors to the area had experienced. They simply didn't feel welcome at restaurants and stores in Farmville. Neither did the Free Schools staff. When an integrated group of teachers went to get ice cream in town, young White men harassed them.[139] Other teachers were afraid of cars or trucks following them when they drove on country roads. But they weren't going to be intimidated.

One group of Free School teachers formed a chorus and gave small concerts. Others organized a basketball team. They played chess and started book clubs. Friendships developed among teachers and staff from different places, different backgrounds, and different racial identities. True integration was there for everyone in Prince Edward to see, whether they wanted to pay attention or not.

• • •

September became October and then November. Teachers and students settled into a routine of hard work. Then suddenly, just before Thanksgiving, violent tragedy struck the nation. President John F. Kennedy was assassinated—shot while he was riding in a motorcade in Dallas, Texas, on a sunny Friday afternoon.

Americans could hardly breathe. No one knew what to say. The news seemed unreal, impossible. Millions of people all over the country and the world watched on television as the president's widow stepped off the plane that had brought her back to Washington later that day, her pink suit stained with her husband's blood. They cried for her and for the Kennedys' children, just six and three years old.

The loss was especially hard for Black Americans who had placed so much hope in Kennedy. Many had seen him as a friend to their cause. For the Black community in Prince Edward County, the president's murder was a particularly terrible blow. They felt a personal connection to Kennedy through the Free Schools. Kennedy's vice president, Lyndon B. Johnson, had been sworn in as president less than two hours after JFK's death. Johnson had grown up in Texas and had represented Texans as a member of Congress for twelve years. Would President Johnson, a White man who spoke with a deep drawl, go forward on civil rights? Did he even know about Prince Edward County? Or was the president's death both a tragedy for the nation and his family, and one more giant step backward for the county's Black children?

Teachers tried to help students understand what had happened, though no one understood *why* it had happened. Two weeks later, students held a ceremony to honor Kennedy. They made a big scroll with a brief message for Mrs. Kennedy. Then every child in the Free Schools signed it. President Kennedy had said the Free Schools should be a model for educating children anywhere in the country who faced the kinds of obstacles children in Prince Edward County did. Students and teachers there would move forward as a tribute to him.

Six months later, word came that Attorney General Robert Kennedy was planning to visit Prince Edward County. Excitement bubbled through the Free Schools. Students were eager to meet Robert Kennedy and show their appreciation for what he had done to get them back into school. They organized to collect pennies for a donation to the John F. Kennedy Memorial Library being built in Boston. Pennies wouldn't make for a big donation, and some children could donate far more. But even pennies were a sacrifice for those children at the Free Schools who lived in poverty, and it was important that every child be able to contribute.

White as well as Black residents of Prince Edward,

US Attorney General Robert Kennedy speaks to a gathering in August 1964. RFK was instrumental in establishing the Free Schools.

and a big group of students from all-White Longwood College, turned out to greet the attorney general. Kennedy looked surprised at this welcome from White townspeople. His staff had tried to arrange a place for him to speak in town but had been turned down everywhere, including at Longwood. However, Neil Sullivan and others in Prince Edward thought something had changed in the county after President Kennedy died. The garbage and late-night calls at the Sullivans' house had stopped. Teachers weren't harassed in town anymore. And Longwood College invited Free School faculty members, Black and White, to use their library. Even better, a number of students from Hampden-Sydney College, about two miles outside of Farmville, volunteered to do after-school tutoring.

Robert Kennedy shook hands and made a few remarks to the crowd, but he was in Farmville for the Free Schools. Oreatha Wiley years later remembered that day in May. She'd been chosen to present Mr. Kennedy with the money her school had collected. She stood in front of the other students, their parents, and two busloads of reporters. Her own parents and her grandfather were there. She said, "When I was walking up to Robert Kennedy, I heard Granddaddy say loudly: 'Yeeeeaaah, that's my granddaughter.' I won't forget that day."[140] Robert Kennedy was delighted with the $99.94 the children had collected. That kind of donation probably meant more to him than $99,000 from a big corporation. His visit meant more to the children than they could say.

The school year was flying by. Everyone agreed that the challenges had been enormous. Several older students had quit, and many younger children were still far behind where they should have been. They might never catch up. But people watching the Free Schools from outside the county saw the students' achievements. Journalists thought the Free Schools were Virginia's most important news story all year. And a number of educators around the country looked at the schools as a model for their communities, especially those where many students lived in poverty.

Over the course of the year, a lot of students did remarkably well, with some picking up two grade levels from where they'd started. Twenty-three young people completed requirements for high school graduation, and nearly half of those had college plans. Another third had jobs waiting. Even students who didn't get up to grade level benefited. Children who'd never used a crayon discovered artistic talent they hadn't known they had. Children who'd never read a book now borrowed piles of library books. At the very least, the children stopped sliding further and further behind.

Teachers and administrators pushed academics as hard as they could. Many students chose to come early and stay late for extra help. But there's more to education than academics, and the Free School administration understood that. Older students could join after-school activities, including sports teams, a band, and student government. Some earned money with jobs in the cafeteria or library— jobs they could not have in the Prince Edward community. And there were weekend field trips.

Imagine being a child of fourteen or fifteen who'd never been more than a few miles from rural Prince Edward County. Imagine going to New York City, where the streets are lined with skyscrapers, and hundreds of people crowd together on every corner waiting for traffic lights to change. Imagine visiting the Empire State Building, the tallest building in the world at the time. How would a child even begin to describe such a trip? Students went to Washington to see the Lincoln Memorial and watch members of Congress debate. They went to their state capitol in Richmond, and to Williamsburg. Those trips were an education in themselves.

Most Americans at the time thought of education as reading, writing, arithmetic, and perhaps some history and citizenship or job skills training. But public schools are also a lifeline for poor children and a safe space for children living in difficult circumstances. Had Prince Edward County officials thought about that when they'd closed their public schools?

Children from the poorest families looked healthier as they ate nutritious lunches every day. They didn't always get enough food at home, and the milk they got at school prevented rickets, a disease that weakens bones. At first, though, many children who lived in very isolated areas tended to catch everything—from colds to chicken pox— from their schoolmates. They needed to be around other children to build immunity. It would take time, but they'd grow stronger. The superintendent brought in dentists and doctors to care for children who'd never had medical attention before. And attendance improved when boxes and boxes of donated clothing arrived. Some children hadn't owned winter coats or boots and had stayed home under the covers on cold days.[141] In all sorts of ways, those children had suffered terribly without public schools.

Almost everyone in the Black community felt good about the Free Schools. The schools showed that people around the country—teachers, corporations that donated tens of thousands of dollars, small businesses, clubs, and individuals who sent books and crayons and contributions—cared about what happened in a tiny, rural piece of Virginia.[142] As Reverend Griffin wrote in a letter to William vanden Heuvel, "What these schools did for the morale of the Negro community can not be measured." But while Griffin praised the Free Schools, he was realistic about the situation. "One would have to be awfully naïve to expect that any one agency could solve in a year's time problems which have been existing in this county for generations."[143]

A year's time. One year. That was the agreement. And that's as far as the donations from businesses, foundations, teacher organizations, and individuals would go. As days grew longer and warmer in the spring of 1964, students and parents worried about what would happen when the Free Schools had to close in August. All eyes were on the US Supreme Court.

CHAPTER 12

DAMAGED VICTORY

1964–1969

T aking a brisk walk through molasses."[144] That's how Jean Fairfax of the AFSC described working with the federal government. The courts were even worse. NAACP lawyers had been fighting for desegregated public education in Prince Edward County since 1951—thirteen years. Think of that. Thirteen years. Many of the children now at the Free Schools hadn't even been born when Oliver Hill and Spottswood Robinson had met with Barbara Johns and the other strikers in 1951. Or when the Supreme Court ruled in 1954 that segregation in public schools was unconstitutional. Or in 1955 when the court said that districts must desegregate "with all deliberate speed." Since then, little by little, districts in many parts of the county had put Black and White students in the same schools at least to some extent, though many Southern states found ways to avoid integration until the late 1960s. In other areas, segregated neighborhoods kept Black and White residents apart in every way. But only Prince Edward County had closed its public schools entirely for five years.

Segregationists in Prince Edward argued that they wanted Black children to have an education. They had closed the schools to defend the US Constitution against tyranny and a federal government that wanted to go outside its powers to tell people and states what to do, they said. J. Barrye Wall wrote in the *Farmville Herald*, "We can devise another system of education, but, once lost, we cannot retrieve a Constitution."[145] Did he and others like him believe that the Constitution was in danger? Did they believe what they said about tyranny? They may have been sincere. Sincere or not, their arguments were a clever way to justify ignoring a Supreme Court decision they didn't like. Segregationists claimed that they were acting as true American patriots. But it's easy to use patriotic and idealistic words to cover up selfish, un-American thoughts. What about the harm they were doing to the children of true American patriots who happened to be Black?

Prince Edward County's attorneys argued in court that the US Constitution does not say that local or state governments have to provide public schools. And the federal government has no power to tell a state or county that it must tax its people and use the money in a certain way. The attorneys said they were protecting state sovereignty—a state's independence and rights. A state's right to do what?

NAACP lawyers argued that the Constitution doesn't need to be that specific. Closing public schools and using tax credits and vouchers for a Whites-only private school left Black and poor White children with no opportunity for an education at all. No state had the right to treat some of its people one way and some another. Such action violated the Fourteenth Amendment's guarantee that no state will deny its citizens "equal protection of the laws."

In December 1963, the Virginia Supreme Court, the highest court in the state, had ruled against the NAACP. Since local officials controlled public schools and Virginia no longer had a law saying that parents had to send their children to school, the Prince Edward County Board of Supervisors could, indeed, close public schools (by then, a court had already banned the use of taxpayer money for vouchers to a private, segregated school). The NAACP appealed to the only court that could overrule a state supreme court—the US Supreme Court. Now, in the days after Robert Kennedy's visit, Prince Edward County's Black community waited for that court's ruling.

Long before sunrise on Monday, March 30, 1964, five of the Free Schools' most accomplished high school students, their teachers, and principal boarded a bus and started off through an early spring snow for Washington, DC. They were going to sit in the chamber as the nine justices of the US Supreme Court heard the case of *Griffin v. County School Board of Prince Edward County*, named for the student listed first among those suing the county—L. Francis (Skip)

Griffin. The reverend's oldest son was one of the brightest young people at the Free Schools. Longwood College's Gordon Moss, the "conscience of the White community,"[146] made the trip too, and so did Neil Sullivan. Segregationist J. Barrye Wall was there as well.

Neil Sullivan wrote later that Wall was a Southern gentleman. Always polite when they ran across each other in town. Sullivan acknowledged that in the Letters to the Editor column in the newspaper, Wall regularly printed opinions from people who opposed segregation. And the publisher never suggested or openly approved of violence.

He didn't call anyone names or hurl insults at Black or White neighbors. But looking at him in that Supreme Court chamber, Sullivan thought that J. Barrye Wall had to know the harm he'd caused. Surely, he had to see what his racist opinions had done to so many families.

William vanden Heuvel, who'd worked so hard to establish the Free Schools, did not attend the Supreme Court hearing that morning. But he had written an essay for the National Education Association's journal in which he said that education was "the very foundation stone" of American society. He went on,

> Free public education means that no child is born a prisoner of any class, that the chains of poverty do not hang forever upon him, and that

the opportunities of a free and open society are
ours and our children's and our grandchildren's.
That is what was taken away from the children
of Prince Edward County.[147]

Would the justices agree that education for all was the
"foundation stone" of American society? Wall, Sullivan,
Moss, and the students followed every word as the lawyers for one side and then the other made their arguments
and the justices asked hard questions. The spectators knew
what segregationists thought, and they knew what they
themselves thought. But what would the justices say when
they made their ruling? Had Prince Edward County violated the Fourteenth Amendment by closing its public
schools to avoid desegregation? And could the court tell
the county to collect taxes and fund public schools? What
would the court's decision mean for public schools around
the country?

On May 25, 1964, the US Supreme Court handed down
its opinion. "Virginia law, as here applied, unquestionably
treats the school children of Prince Edward differently
from the way it treats the school children of all other Virginia counties." That was a violation of the Fourteenth
Amendment. The decision went on to say that ordering the county to collect taxes for schools "is within the

court's power." Prince Edward County had to open and desegregate its public schools.

The long court battle was over. When other Southern states and counties heard about the ruling in the Prince Edward case, they did not attempt to shut down their own public schools. They knew they couldn't win. But another piece of the struggle was about to begin.

"If schools are opened on a desegregated basis next September, how good will they be?"[148] It was a fair question. A critical question. Betty Carter, a student editor for the Free Schools' high school newspaper was right to ask it. Only the Prince Edward County Board of Supervisors could answer.

When the schools reopened in September 1964, the Free Schools children would still need reading specialists, speech therapists, and math tutors. They'd need small classes, experienced teachers, individualized plans, and lots of encouragement. The public schools would have to do everything the Free Schools had done and more. It was the only way to even begin to repair the damage.

However, most of Prince Edward's school board members and the powerful White supremacists who influenced them had no intention of doing anything with any real meaning. Their goal was to keep White students at the private academy and Black students in the public schools, just as if the schools were still segregated by law. They were certain that very few White families would send their children to the public schools, especially if those schools were as unappealing as possible.

The county budgeted $564,000 for schools in the 1964–65 school year. Of that, less than one third went to the public schools. Over two thirds went to the Whites-only Prince

Betty Carter attended the Free Schools in 1963-64 and graduated from the desegregated and renamed Prince Edward County High School in 1966.

Edward Academy through tuition vouchers. Leaders actually handed the voucher money out in the middle of the night before officials at the court of appeals could hear about what they were doing and stop them. On average, the county spent $118 on each public school child and $239 on each Prince Edward Academy child. Would that money give the public schools the resources they needed?

Remedial reading? No.

Money for special needs? No.

Small classes? No.

Excellent teachers from other parts of the country? No.

A class on Black history? No.

College preparation courses? No.

Nutritious meals in the cafeteria? No.

The board also refused to order any new books or equipment for the reopening schools and waited until the last minute to recruit teachers. Only half of the people they hired were actually certified to teach. Worse, the board didn't even bother to interview everyone they employed, allowing complete strangers to go into classrooms with the county's children.[149]

Two months after the schools reopened, Reverend Griffin wrote to William vanden Heuvel, who was back with the International Rescue Committee in New York. Griffin thanked vanden Heuvel again for working so hard to set up the Free Schools and then got to his point.

For five years our community was without any public schools, and because of this a generation of our children are permanently crippled and disabled.

After thirteen years of litigation we have only succeeded in reopening a type of public

school system vastly inferior to the one in exis-
tence in 1959.

The School Board takes the attitude that
education for Negro children in Prince Edward
County is a privilege, not a right.[150]

Once more, Prince Edward County's White supremacist leaders had defied the intention of a Supreme Court
ruling, doled out tax money to people they approved of
while showing no concern for anyone else, and defended
their actions as noble and patriotic. How were their
actions saving Prince Edward County and the country from tyranny? How exactly was it noble and patriotic to defy the Supreme Court, violate the Fourteenth
Amendment, and damage the lives of 1,500 American
children?

Nancy Adams had come to Prince Edward County in
1963 to take over leadership of the American Friends
Service Committee programs there. She reported on the
public schools after they reopened in 1964. They were terribly overcrowded, she said. The school board didn't want
to spend money on repairs and equipment for the public
schools, so they opened only the four buildings the Free
Schools had already repaired and equipped. Some elementary school classrooms had forty children with one

teacher. High school classes weren't much better. And those teachers no one had interviewed? Children went home with stories of their teachers calling them "n_____."

The schools had no program to help students who'd fallen behind, and Adams saw children of ten, eleven, and twelve unable to complete first-grade assignments. If they didn't get help very soon, they'd never be able to catch up.[151] At the same time, capable high school students couldn't take the courses they needed to get into college. The school didn't offer those courses and didn't offer drama or art or other common high school classes. Adams also reported that the cafeteria was inadequate, running out of food almost every day.

Teachers described a terrible lack of organization at the schools. They had to sort through piles of random books and supplies to find what they needed for their classes. They had no meetings for setting goals or planning. Middle school and high school teachers had advanced students and students who couldn't read at all in the same class. And as one teacher said of herself and other upper-grade teachers, "None of us have the faintest idea of how to teach anyone how to read."[152]

Students who'd gone to the Free Schools for a year were horribly disappointed. Where was the excitement and enthusiasm they'd seen at the Free Schools? Where were the teachers who'd worked so hard to help them?

One high school student reported that some teachers let students sit and talk for at least half of their class time. They assigned homework but never checked it. Other high schoolers complained that teachers wouldn't let students discuss difficult topics like slavery or civil rights even in history and government classes. Administrators didn't monitor the halls or try to keep order, and every day brought more chaos.[153]

Neil Sullivan wrote that "disciplinary problems were almost nonexistent" at the Free Schools.[154] Now one student described her schoolmates—the very same students she'd known at the Free Schools—as "wild. Like they didn't have no self-control . . . Everything is upside-down."[155]

Nancy Adams agreed that everything was upside down. Like Jean Fairfax, she believed that some White people in the county supported desegregation but were afraid to say so. She organized a group of about fifty Black and some White citizens who were concerned about the reopening of the public schools. Citizens for Public Education (CPE) met as an integrated group. But when they went to see school officials, they accomplished almost nothing. The superintendent even told the group that how the county ran the schools was not their business.[156] Imagine that. How could a public school superintendent tell citizens that what he did was not their business? Their taxes paid his salary. And when CPE members discovered that the school board had changed meeting times and places to avoid talking to them, to hide from them, it certainly seemed that everything was upside down.

Think about the frustration of trying to deal with a school board that didn't believe education mattered or that Black children's futures mattered. A school board that would hide to avoid talking to parents. A high school junior said, "They could have given us much better schools and teachers, if they wanted to. But what they want to do is get these kids on out of school without much education and put more in. They just want cheap labor."[157] Gordon Moss had made the same accusation a few years earlier.

No one in the Black community was surprised by the county officials' actions. It was an old story in Prince Edward County (and in many other places). Between 1964 and 1967, the public schools limped along—overcrowded, poorly equipped, underfunded. Many older students left school before graduation, giving Prince Edward County the highest dropout rate in the state. Reading scores stayed low, and attendance was poor. Even so, the majority of students didn't give up. When the county offered a summer school program, about 60 percent of the public school students signed on. Many students and parents also became more active in the politics of Prince Edward County's public schools.

In late September 1968, the school board refused almost every request made in a petition signed by more than a thousand adults in the county. High school students responded by staging a walkout to show their support for the petition and to demand a voice for Black citizens in school decisions. They soon went back to class, but the situation simmered for several months. It boiled over in April 1969, when the school board completed a report that blamed the tensions over the schools on Black leaders and new ideas of *Black Power*—a part of the civil rights movement that emphasized Black pride and defiance of White power.[158]

Most students in high school in 1969 hadn't been alive when Barbara Johns led the 1951 strike. But they had suffered through the lockout and now went to a substandard school. Like Barbara, they were fed up. They were fed up with the poor education and with the poor equipment and supplies. And they were furious that the school board had decided against keeping a well-qualified, dedicated English teacher—Burwell Robinson—on the faculty. He would not be back in the fall. Why? The school board didn't say. But Robinson, one of just six White teachers at the high school, had encouraged his students to express their feelings about the school and the county and the injustice they faced every day. Reverend Griffin claimed that Robinson's flaw was "just being a normal person that doesn't find any trouble working with black people."[159]

On April 23, 1969—the eighteenth anniversary of the student strike at the old Moton High School—Prince Edward County's Black high school students once again walked out in protest. This time, they were striking against the poor quality of their education at Prince Edward

Travis Harris struggled with academics when the Free Schools opened. He persevered, and graduated from the newly integrated Moton High School in 1968 at the age of twenty.

County High School (housed in the 1953 Moton High School building and renamed when the county desegregated and reopened the school in 1964). They marched two miles into Farmville to demonstrate at the county courthouse. The strike continued until Monday, April 28. "We're not rioting and we don't consider ourselves black militants," one student told a reporter at a crowded meeting that night. "We're students. We are against the white stronghold on the school board."[160]

Like the strikers in 1951, the students were peaceful. They demanded a new superintendent, Black representation on the school board, a better gym, better books, and more. They didn't get everything they asked for, and Burwell Robinson was not rehired. But

Anthony Farley attended the Free Schools and graduated from Moton High School in 1969.

in late May, the school board decided not to renew the unpopular superintendent's contract. He would not be back. That was good news. Other changes came more slowly, but they came. Perhaps Prince Edward County could make progress, could move in a new direction.

J. Barrye Wall hoped that wasn't so. He didn't want any new directions and said, "If it were up to me, I'd close the schools again."[161] Fortunately, it wasn't up to him. The majority of White residents of Prince Edward remained segregationists. But they realized that the country was changing, and they were ready to accept some desegregation in some places as long as it didn't change their lives. When two Black men received appointments to the school board, White board members admitted that those men had valuable insights and opinions. Outside the schools, the sheriff's department hired six Black part-time deputies, and the police department gained a Black police officer. A few other positions opened to Black county residents as well. All that was still a small drop in the big bucket of what was needed, but it was progress.[162]

Real improvement in the schools came after another new school superintendent arrived in Prince Edward. By then, the state was writing a new constitution to replace the segregationist 1902 document. And a new governor had issued a policy that required counties, including Prince Edward, to give their public schools more money. Superintendent James Anderson was ready to spend that money on what mattered most. Before long, reading and math scores went up, the dropout rate went down, and more White families chose to send their children to the public schools.

Equality was a long way off, and defeating racism was still only a dream. But Prince Edward County had weathered several terrible storms, and its Black community had proved brave and resilient. Even so, healing, if it happened at all, would take a very long time.

CHAPTER 13

FACING THE PAST

1980–1998

M ost people in Prince Edward County didn't talk about it. Thirty and forty years later, they didn't talk about the court cases or the school closings or anything connected to that painful past. White residents didn't discuss the part they or their parents or grandparents had played in the closings. Most didn't say how they felt about it even years later. White children at the Prince Edward Academy in the 1980s and 1990s didn't know that some of their grandparents had helped lock Black children out of school. They didn't know that their private school, the same school many of their parents had attended, had been founded in the first place to avoid desegregation. And they didn't know about the pain, heartache, and resentment so many Black adults carried with them. No one talked about it.

Black residents had their own reasons for not talking about the closings. Strike leader John Stokes had a long career as an educator, but it was fifty years before he decided to write about the 1951 strike. He had a hard

time with "things that are painful for me to think about."
He saw that some people who were later locked out of
school blamed the strikers for what happened. "I didn't
want to . . . stir up more resentment."[163]

Those students who had suffered the most didn't want
to admit later that they couldn't help their children with
homework. They'd spent years hiding the fact that they
couldn't read. As Hilton Lee, Sr., said, "It would always
hurt me as a father when my children would come and ask
me something about their homework and I couldn't help
them."[164] Those who'd made it through school on time or
finished years later didn't want to discuss the sorrow they
still felt. Dorothy Lee Allen said, "I don't often talk about
the era of the school closing . . . because it makes me cry,
it saddens me, even forty-five years later. . . . I think about
how much I missed in life . . . all of my girlhood dreams,
visions, and hopes."[165]

Betty Jean Ward, who told Superintendent Sullivan in
1963 that the Free Schools would be her family's salvation,
was one of the young people arrested that summer on the
steps of the all-White Farmville Baptist Church. Forty
years had passed, and she still couldn't go into that church.
"I'll never forget what happened," she said. "I'm trying to
forgive."[166] Many Black children in Prince Edward in the
1980s and 1990s had no idea that their parents had been
locked out of school for years. No idea that many of them

felt anger or frustration even decades later. Those children learned about Rosa Parks and Martin Luther King, Jr., and never realized that their own mothers and fathers were part of that story of perseverance and courage. No one talked about it.

One day in 1995, an opportunity arose. An opportunity to confront the past, and to start a real conversation about what had happened and why. That opportunity involved the very building where everything had started forty-four years earlier—the original 1939 R. R. Moton High School building where Barbara Johns had organized the student strike in 1951.

When the county built the new Moton High School for Black students in 1953, the 1939 building had become a Black elementary school. Once the schools closed, it sat empty until the Free Schools had rented it in 1963. When the county's public schools had reopened and desegregated in 1964, the building had again housed an elementary school.

Now, in 1995, the school board planned to move students to another school building and sell or tear down the 1939 structure. But some people opposed that idea, especially members of a local organization of Black women. The Martha E. Forrester Council was part of the National Council of Negro Women and named for a Farmville teacher who had devoted her life to improving education for Black children in Prince Edward County. Many members of the group had been students or teachers at Moton. They thought the building should be preserved as a visible reminder of civil rights history. The old R. R. Moton High School should be a nationally registered historic building.

James Ghee, a lawyer and the local NAACP president (the position Reverend Griffin had held during the 1950s), had been locked out of Prince Edward's schools as a teenager in 1959. He went to the training centers at first and then to his grandparents' home in a neighboring county. Two years into the closings, he traveled a thousand miles to a family in Iowa with the AFSC placement program. "The father was Italian. The mother was Japanese and had been in concentration [internment] camps in America during World War II and was hell-bent on making sure no one discriminated against me," he said. "She wouldn't allow a white barber in Iowa City to refuse to cut my hair."[167] Instead, she learned how to cut Ghee's hair herself.

Ghee was the only Black student in his class at school. He put any discomfort aside and worked hard to do well. He stayed in Iowa for college and then came back to the University of Virginia for law school as one of the school's first Black students. Then he returned to Farmville as the first Black lawyer in Prince Edward County.

James Ghee went to a family in Iowa when the schools closed, and later became the first Black attorney in Prince Edward County.

When the issue of the old high school came up, James Ghee worked to save the building. He didn't want to see the Moton story swept away. He believed that the people of Prince Edward—all of them—needed to talk about the past. "Until we are able to talk across racial lines," he said, "we are going to have this thing fester."[168]

Ghee and others who agreed with him suggested turning the old high school into a civil rights museum. Members of the county board of supervisors argued that leaving the building standing would be a constant reminder of a difficult time. A time they preferred to forget or ignore or hide. Museum supporters, including the new editor of the *Farmville Herald*, stood firm.

J. Barrye Wall, the segregationist owner of the *Herald*, had died in 1985. His sons now owned and ran the paper but didn't write the editorials, as their father had. Ken Woodley had that job. Woodley had grown up in Richmond and had been part of a small minority of White students in a largely Black school. He'd never thought much about race and had never heard of massive resistance when he'd gone to work for the paper in 1979.

Though he'd just graduated from Hampden-Sydney College, only a few miles down the road, he'd had no idea that Prince Edward's schools had been closed or that the newspaper had a long racist, segregationist history. He'd been shocked to learn that the "kind elderly gentleman" who still came to the office every day was a White supremacist and a leader of massive resistance.[169]

Woodley hadn't been sure he could still work for Wall on the paper and thought about quitting his job. But something told him not to run away from the ugly past. He stayed, and a few years after Wall's death, he'd begun writing opinion pieces and then had become the paper's editor. When county officials proposed tearing down the old high school, Woodley wrote,

> If we're going to tear down the former R. R. Moton High School . . . let's go ahead and tear down Independence Hall [in Philadelphia, where the Declaration of Independence and US Constitution were signed]. . . . The Farmville school building is no less a monument to human courage in the belief that all human beings are created equal.[170]

In the days that followed, the paper got no complaints from readers, and both Black and White residents said they liked the idea of a museum. It was time to face Prince Edward's past. So many feelings shoved away. So many stories untold. A museum could tell those stories of courage, of determination, and of the importance of public education. It could tell stories of triumph in the face of terrible obstacles. And the wounds that never healed.

• • •

Warren (Ricky) Brown could share one of those stories. Heartbroken at six when the school bus didn't come, Ricky had finally started first grade when he was ten years old. He felt out of place and angry and nearly quit. But he was a good athlete, and football, basketball, and baseball kept him in school. If Ricky had had a normal education all those years, he probably would have gone to college on a sports scholarship. Though he graduated from high school on time, however, he knew he wouldn't be able to do college-level work. Instead Ricky found a job with the state prison system. Even there, his reading and writing skills weren't good enough, and he started teaching himself. But when he went to work for an electric company and had to complete training classes, he said he felt like "I was behind everyone else in the class . . . mainly young men who had just graduated from high school."

Eventually, Brown became a resource officer for the Prince Edward Middle School in the same school district that had locked him out years earlier. He understood that, all these years later, the effects of the school closings harmed the children of students like him, whose education had been interrupted or cut off. They couldn't help their children with school. Brown started a program for those children. As he said, "When a mother or father has no education, it's a strong possibility that they will not talk to their children about education. . . . Those children probably will not stress education to their children and so on for generations."[171] Think about that. How many children would continue to be harmed by what the segregationists had done?

John Hurt, who found the Free Schools "impossible" after four years at home, had a story too. He had heartache as well. Hurt didn't really understand how much harm the school closings had done until he grew older. "Many, many people couldn't read and write, and you almost thought it was natural. But it was when we would visit other counties and be around people our age that we realized how damaged we were." In his mid-twenties, he hired a reading tutor who came to his house twice a week. "It was a struggle!" he said. But he stuck with it for years, no matter how hard it was. "How could a people be so evil as to do something like close the schools?" he asked. "They did not only deny me, they denied my children."[172] "It would have been better if they had cut off my arm or leg. . . . I could have got by with one arm or no arms. But the thing they took, it's priceless."[173]

Travis Harris had worked like a grown man while the schools had been closed and finished high school when he was twenty. It had been a long, difficult road. Harris served in the military, as many young Black men from Prince Edward County did, and later worked as a police

John Hurt boards a Prince Edward County school bus to help lead a rally in Richmond to support the *Brown v. Board of Education* Scholarship Program. Locked out of school, Hurt refused to give up on education.

officer at the state capitol in Richmond. He returned to Farmville for a job in the sheriff's department and earned several promotions over the next twenty years. In 1999, Travis Harris won election as the first Black sheriff of Prince Edward County.[174] Consider what that meant for him and for the Black community. Still, even that kind of victory didn't heal the hurt completely.

Dorothy Lee Allen had wanted to become a registered nurse. But the schools closed before she finished high school. She was twenty-one years old and a mother when the Free Schools finally opened. She couldn't go back to finish at that point. Twenty-five years later, Allen finally earned her GED—a certificate similar to a high school diploma. She then trained as a nursing assistant, but that was as close as she could get to fulfilling her dream. Becoming a registered nurse requires a college degree, and the school closings had put college out of Dorothy Lee Allen's reach.[175] Did her patients see how much more Dorothy could have done? She might have been an accomplished nurse in a place that needed more nurses. She might have trained other nurses to fill even more needs. She might have saved lives. Like Travis Harris and so many others, Dorothy Lee Allen survived and made a good life. But the school closings would never be over for her. The past was still there in the present.

Several young adults who never learned to read proficiently still managed to set up their own small businesses or work in trades like carpentry or mechanics and did well. Some farmed. Others got a late education and built new lives. But questions always remained. As one locked-out student said, "You have to live the rest of your life wondering who you could have been or what you could have done with your life."[176] People in 1995, Black and White, needed to hear that.

. . .

The children and teens who left the county to go to school during the closings generally succeeded academically and professionally. One young man became a dentist, and others like James Ghee became lawyers. Several went into teaching or government work. But they were only a very small percentage of the Black children in the county during those years. And their victories didn't protect them from pain. Family separations and financial stress and struggle left lasting scars. Many felt guilt that they'd had opportunities that their friends and neighbors—and sometimes their brothers and sisters—hadn't had. And it hurt to know that a big part of the community they came from hadn't cared what happened to them.

Angeles Wood and her sister went to relatives in New Jersey for two years and then came home when the Free Schools opened. Angeles went on to college and graduate school and became a teacher in Prince Edward County. But she admitted that she didn't remember her time away from home. "I don't know how I have managed to block it out. I can't see anybody, teachers or students, in my mind. Nothing is there."[177]

Sylvia Oliver's family gave up running water and indoor toilets to rent a house so she and her sisters could go to school. That sacrifice allowed her to finish high school on time, but the struggle stayed with her. "To people who will read this story one hundred years from now, I want them to know that the worst thing you can do to children is to deny them an education."[178]

Some of the locked-out students became activists as a result of their experience. Skip Griffin, the reverend's son, went to New Jersey and then to Newton, Massachusetts, for school, and excelled. He went on to college at Harvard, became a civil rights activist there, and later served as a director of the African American Institute at Northeastern University.[179]

Moses Scott lived with a Holocaust survivor in Massachusetts while going to high school, and then went to Howard University in Washington, DC, and eventually to Harvard Business School. Those credentials were impressive, but Scott considered his greatest accomplishment "finishing high school."[180] Imagine how close Scott came to losing all those opportunities at Howard and Harvard. Imagine how close the business world came to losing his talents.

Most of the students who went away were grateful for the experience. It changed their lives for the better. They grew up quickly, and got to know people they would never have known at home. Some even met their future spouses while they were away. But many carried memories like the one Jo Ann Randall described: "I can still see the look on my mother's face and in my father's eyes when they had to send us away and didn't know what to say."[181]

As the twentieth century came to a close, it was time to honor the sacrifice that parents like that had made for their children. Time to recognize the pain that those children carried with them. Time for the White community to gain understanding of what the closings had done to their Black neighbors.

Perhaps a museum could help White residents see the past through their Black neighbors' eyes. Perhaps it could show people everywhere the kind of senseless damage that White supremacy causes. Perhaps a museum could honor the many victories that the locked-out generation had won despite their painful scars. It was time to tell Prince Edward's whole story. It was also time to recognize the impact that Prince Edward's story had had on the United States.

The students who'd gone on strike in 1951 deserved recognition. They had joined the lawsuit—*Brown v. Board of Education*—that had resulted in the end of legal public school segregation in the United States. What they had done mattered. They had changed the country.

It was time to recognize the resilience of those who'd been shut out of school from 1959 to 1964. With the Supreme Court's ruling in their lawsuit—*Griffin v. County School Board of Prince Edward County*—they'd saved public education in the United States. No state or county could again pick and choose who would go to school and

The former Robert Russa Moton High School in Farmville, Virginia, is now a National Historic Landmark and opened as a museum in 2001.

who would not. The students' perseverance mattered.

It was also time to tell Prince Edward County's White community the truth. The young people of the 1990s weren't responsible for what their parents and grandparents thought or what actions they'd taken, good or bad. But those young people deserved to know the truth. They *needed* to know what had happened and why, if Prince Edward was ever going to recover. They needed to know, if they were going to crack the cycle of White supremacy that had hurt so many people.

A museum was a good place to start.

The board of supervisors finally agreed to sell the old high school to the Martha E. Forrester Council of women, though several board members still wanted to tear it down. In 1995, the National Register of Historic Places listed the building as one of the country's significant cultural sites. That would protect it from destruction in the future. It became a national historic landmark under the National Park Service in 1998.

There was a long way to go and there were many questions to be answered, but something important had begun.

CHAPTER 14

UNFINISHED BUSINESS

2001–2020

S mall steps. On April 23, 2001—the fiftieth anniversary of the student strike that started it all—the doors opened at the Robert Russa Moton Museum. Sermons in Farmville's Black and White churches that Sunday focused on race relations and healing. Nearly a thousand people attended the museum's opening ceremony. Guests included attorney Oliver Hill, strike leader John Stokes, and many other Black students from the 1951 strike, the school closings, and beyond. Younger Black residents came to the ceremony, and so did a lot of White residents.

More events followed over the next few years. Students who'd gone on strike and students who'd been locked out came together for the ceremonies commemorating what had happened when they were young. Many had left the county and never moved back, but they visited to honor the sacrifices they'd all made. They talked about their pain and about their feelings of connection to the county despite everything. Several former students had plans to return

John Stokes and Ken Woodley at the Prince Edward
County Courthouse after a celebration of the fiftieth
anniversary of the Moton High School student strike.

and build houses on land their families still owned. Others
came back to care for elderly parents or be closer to family.
Whether they had moved away or stayed in Prince Edward,
whether they wanted to live in the county or not, hundreds
of Black men and women from Prince Edward County felt
that they had "unfinished business" there.[182]

A lot of White people who'd grown up in Prince
Edward also had unfinished business. Marcie Wall
remembered hearing loud arguments in her house as her

father, J. Barrye Wall's son, supported closing the schools and her mother strongly opposed the idea. They weren't the only White family caught in those arguments. Husbands and wives argued; older and younger generations argued. They weren't torn apart the way Black families were, but the closings had caused financial and emotional strain all over the county.

Many young White children who didn't hear discussions in 1959 were adults before they knew that their parents or grandparents had played key roles in the school closings or had disagreed on what to do. How did they feel when they found out that a beloved grandfather who'd played games with them and bounced them on his knee had been a racist, a segregationist, a founder of the Defenders of State Sovereignty and Individual Liberties? In many cases, that grandparent was gone and it was too late to ask for an explanation. Those who did get explanations often heard "I was taking care of my children" or "What else could I do?"

And what about the White children in the county who didn't go to the academy? John Hines, who never went back to school after seventh grade, worked hard and used his experience on the farm and in the army as his education. He started a logging company and a trucking business and did well. But he saw that younger children who had barely learned to read and write had very limited opportunities

John Hines holds his young son. Despite not finishing school, Hines started a successful trucking company and logging business.

in life. Like Gordon Moss and others, Hines believed that a handful of older, powerful people in the county was responsible for the school closings. Did those people regret what they'd done?[183]

Some older White residents felt sorrow for what they or others had done all those years ago, and some didn't. Robert Taylor had been on the board of the Prince Edward Academy from the beginning. Fifty years later, he was proud that most White children had never had to miss any school. He pointed out that White parents had made big financial sacrifices to send their children to school. What about Black children? Was there anything about that time that he regretted? "Not a damn thing." Was he still in favor of segregation? "Of course. Always have been."[184] Not everyone wanted to move forward. But it was time.

More steps. In 2003, state lawmakers in Virginia issued a statement of "profound regret over the 1959–1964 closing of the public schools in Prince Edward County, Virginia."[185] County officials then voted to give honorary diplomas to the people who'd never graduated from high school after the closings. About 400 women and men participated in the ceremony. Many others refused. The diplomas were honorary, not real, they said. The diplomas wouldn't help anyone find a job or go to college after all these years. An empty ceremony wouldn't change anything.

Ken Woodley of the *Farmville Herald* thought the state and county should do more. The statement of regret was a good step. So was the honorary graduation. But neither did anything *concrete*. They wouldn't help John Hurt with his reading or take away Jo Ann Randall's traumatic memories. Woodley decided to press for scholarships— money—for the locked-out generation. Money that students harmed by the school closings could use for education even fifty years later. That would be a big step. It took a year of hard work by Woodley and former Prince Edward County students. They talked to legislators, rallied support from the governor and other officials, traveled back and forth to and from Richmond to make their voices heard, and more. Their work paid off. The legislature in Richmond—once the capital of the Confederacy—voted almost unanimously in favor of the *Brown v. Board of Education* Scholarship Program and Fund.

The scholarships became reality in 2005. Once again, Prince Edward County was in the news, but this time the news was good. Since then, at least 250 men and women have used the money for basic adult education programs, community colleges, technical education, college, graduate school, even a PhD.[186] Rita Moseley was one of them.

Rita was twelve when the schools closed. She was lucky enough to continue her education, but the cost was terrible. Her mother found a family who would take Rita in so she could go to school. The family lived over a hundred miles west of Farmville, and Rita hadn't been away from home before. She would never forget seeing her mother drive away while she stayed with strangers. Later she realized that she and her brother lost their close relationship during those years because they didn't finish growing up together and he didn't go to school.[187] But she was glad to at least finish high school and was a secretary at the desegregated Farmville High School for many years.

Moseley worked closely with Ken Woodley to convince the state legislature to fund the scholarship program. Their success opened new doors for her. More than forty-five years after being shut out of school, Rita Moseley earned a bachelor's degree and then a master's degree in executive leadership. "I can see not only the tremendous effect it [the scholarship program] had on my life but it affected and changed other people's lives, where they're now in schools and they're able to get better jobs and they'll be able to look at things in a different way." Those scholarships were the first *reparations*—payments made for past wrongs—in the United States since the modern civil rights movement had begun.[188]

More steps. In 2007, Virginia marked the 400th anniversary of Jamestown, the first permanent English settlement in North America. Visitors commemorated the landing of the British ships, and celebrated the establishment of the first elected legislature in British North America. Lawmakers in Richmond also recognized the event with another statement of "profound regret"—this one for the "involuntary servitude of Africans and the exploitation of Native Americans."[189]

The following year, the state approved building a civil rights memorial. A stone wall now stands on the grounds of Virginia's state capitol. On one side of the large rectangle, bronze statues show Barbara Johns stepping forward from a group of students and adults.

Johns never lived in Prince Edward County again after the

REACHING FOR THE MOON

BARBARA JOHNS

Virginia Civil Rights Memorial, Richmond, with Barbara Johns at the center.

1951 strike. She finished high school in Alabama and went to Spelman College, an historically Black women's college in Atlanta, Georgia. She married, moved to Philadelphia, earned a degree in library science, and raised five children. Her career as a school librarian allowed her to follow her passion for education and reading. Johns's life in Philadelphia was full and happy. But she didn't forget what had happened in Prince Edward County. Thirty-five years after the Johns house burned to the ground, Barbara and her brothers and sister decided to rebuild on the land they still owned. The place where they grew up and where she planned the strike was still important to them. Sadly, Johns never saw the completed house or the civil rights monument in Richmond. She died of cancer in 1991 at the age of fifty-six.

HBCUs

About one hundred of the more than three thousand institutions of higher learning in the United States are identified as Historically Black Colleges and Universities. The Higher Education Act of 1965 defines an HBCU as "any historically black college or university that was established prior to 1964, whose principal mission was, and is, the education of black Americans." Most HBCUs were founded between 1861 and 1900 when very few other colleges accepted Black students. They continue to focus on higher education for Black Americans (about three-fourths of HBCU students are Black), including thousands of low-income, first-generation college students. NAACP attorney Oliver Hill, Supreme Court Justice Thurgood Marshall, Martin Luther King, Jr., Oprah Winfrey, and Vice President Kamala Harris all graduated from HBCUs.

John Stokes also left Prince Edward County and never moved back. He became an award-winning teacher and then a middle school principal in Baltimore. After he retired, he decided to open up about his part in the strike and the significance of *Brown v. Board of Education*. He started speaking about the events of that time and eventually wrote a book for young readers. Stokes knew that his story—the Moton High School story—was important. So was the new memorial. About 4,000 people turned out for the dedication ceremony. They were there to honor members of Prince Edward County's Black community and their struggle for equality. The community's perseverance and courage helped save America's public schools and were a model for younger generations.

A statue of Reverend Francis Griffin stands at

Barbara Johns became a school librarian in Philadelphia and raised five children with her husband, Reverend William Powell.

one end of the stone rectangle at the state capitol. Griffin gave up his plans to leave Prince Edward County all those years ago. He chose to stay because he believed the people of Prince Edward needed him at the time of the strike. They needed him during the terrible school closings and years of struggle for decent schools. Griffin sacrificed his dreams, but his voice carried far beyond the county's borders. He became known as the "fighting preacher" and was a fiery champion for civil rights, tireless in his efforts to achieve equality for all Americans. Griffin died in 1980 at the age of sixty-two, still fighting for equality.

The Virginia Civil Rights Memorial honors Reverend L. Francis Griffin as a champion for children and education.

Statues of NAACP lawyers Spottswood Robinson and Oliver Hill stand at the other end of the wall. Robinson argued civil rights cases before the Supreme Court and then served as dean of the Howard University School of Law. Later he became a member of the US Commission on Civil Rights. He went on to serve as a judge on the US Court of Appeals for the District of Columbia and then as its chief judge, the first Black person to do so. He died in 1998 at eighty-two. Oliver Hill moved from fighting for public school desegregation to fighting for desegregation in public housing. He then spent thirty years as a trial lawyer, focusing on civil rights cases. He also started a foundation to help poor people get legal services. Even in retirement, Hill continued to speak out for equal rights for all. He died in 2007 at the age of one hundred.

Statues of unnamed people stand behind Barbara Johns. An unnamed child stands beside Reverend Griffin. More unnamed people stand on the other side of the memorial wall. Those statues represent the adults and children who suffered for so long. They stand for the Black people of Prince Edward who refused to give in and accept continued

Bronze statues depict NAACP attorneys Oliver Hill, waving a legal brief, and Spottswood Robinson, standing shoulder to shoulder with him.

segregation in their schools. The people who sacrificed to protest the destruction of the county's, and possibly the country's, public schools. Reverend Griffin said, "I'm certain by remaining adamant through the long struggle, Prince Edward blacks saved public education in this nation."[190] That's a legacy to honor.

The memorial in Richmond couldn't do anything to right wrongs or make up for the wounds that Prince Edward

County and the state had inflicted on its Black citizens. But symbols are important. The memorial tells a real story and sends a real message. Ken Woodley wanted Prince Edward County's government to send a message too. The county board of supervisors agreed. They placed a "light of reconciliation" in the courthouse bell tower in Farmville. On the lawn below it, a marker honors the students who went on strike and the students who were locked out. Importantly, the marker includes the words "with sorrow for closing the schools." Sorrow. It wasn't as strong a statement as many Black citizens wanted. But it was an admission that what had happened there shouldn't have.

In 2021, Black residents made up about 33 percent of Prince Edward County's population. About 61 percent of residents were White and not Hispanic, and some 6 percent of residents were of Hispanic, Asian, or other ethnicities. The county's public schools served just over 2,000 students. About 55 percent of those students were Black, about 36 percent were White, and just over 9 percent of students identified as Hispanic, multiracial, Asian, or other ethnicities.

The Prince Edward Academy still existed in 2021, much smaller than it had been and with a new name, new leadership, and new policies since the 1990s. The renamed Fuqua School is open to Black and other minority students, but almost 93 percent of the student population was White in 2021.

The county's public schools today face many of the same problems that all schools face around the country. Those problems or issues are often connected to poverty. In Prince Edward, a lot of that poverty is connected to the school closings sixty years ago. And the county government does not provide the schools with enough money to address all the issues.

Illiteracy in Prince Edward is higher than it is in most of Virginia. As Ricky Brown said, parents who aren't educated don't usually emphasize education for their children. Parents who can't read can't help their children become good readers. And people who can't read well or don't finish high school are often poor because there are so few jobs open to them. So the Prince Edward story goes on.

Even when all of the people who lived in Prince Edward in the 1950s and 1960s are gone, the story won't end because the journey toward justice and equality doesn't end there or anywhere else. Virginia and Prince Edward County are still taking steps toward justice because there is still unfinished business.

At the Robert Russa Moton Museum, people who lived through the 1951 strike and the school closings still meet to discuss their experiences and share their stories. Women and men who went on strike in 1969 do the same.

The museum educates schoolchildren and adults who live in the county as well as those who come from other places to learn more about civil rights history. It provides a space for learning, for discussing and sharing the past, and for confronting that unfinished business. It helps the Prince Edward community and other communities continue to take steps forward.

The state of Virginia continues to take steps forward too. During the early spring of 2020, Virginia's legislature established a Commission for Historical Statues in the United States Capitol. Each state contributes two statues to the US Capitol Building. They commemorate deceased citizens of that state who were important for their "civic or military services." Virginia had contributed its original statues in 1908. That was just after the state adopted its 1902 constitution—the constitution that made segregation the law and allowed the state to take away the civil rights that Black Americans had gained after the Civil War (that constitution was replaced in 1971).

One statue honored Virginian George Washington, the biggest hero of the American Revolution and first president of the United States. Washington made enormous contributions to the founding of the country and set an example of leadership that is still admired today. Washington grew up in Virginia in the 1730s and 1740s. As an adult, he owned thousands of acres of farmland and controlled over three hundred enslaved people. During and after the American Revolution, he began to rethink his beliefs about slavery, though he didn't take action at the time or speak publicly about his beliefs. In his will, however, he freed all the enslaved people that Virginia's laws allowed him to free.

The other statue honored Virginian Robert E. Lee, an enslaver who never spoke publicly against slavery and defended it in writing. As a graduate of the United States Military Academy at West Point and a US Army officer, Lee took an oath to defend the United States against all enemies foreign and domestic (within the country). He was considered an outstanding military leader during the Mexican-American War (1846–1848), and later served as superintendent of West Point. In March 1861, after South Carolina and six other states seceded, Lee was promoted to the rank of colonel and renewed his oath to defend the United States. But when the Civil War started in April, he turned down the offer to lead the Union Army against the secessionist states and resigned from the military. Virginia seceded just days after the fighting began, and Lee was soon named a general in the Confederate Army. He led that army in war against the United States of America. After the Civil War, Lee opposed voting and other civil rights for Black Americans.[191]

In July 2020, Virginia's commission recommended

removing the Lee statue. The state's governor agreed, saying, "The Robert E. Lee statue does not tell our full and true story, and it has never represented all Virginians."[192] The statue is now at the Virginia Museum of History & Culture in Richmond.

Other states, counties, and cities around the country also decided to look at the Confederate statues and monuments that have stood in places of honor for decades. Like the Robert E. Lee statue, those monuments and statues have never represented all of the people. They have never told the full history of the country, and the story they did tell wasn't accurate. Many localities set up citizen committees to consider changes to neighborhood and street names as well. They reconsidered the names of schools and other public buildings, too.

These efforts are symbolic. They don't immediately change lives or heal wounds. But the study and thinking that should go into making changes may result in a greater understanding of the past and the present, and start a healing process. Thoughtfully removing symbols that portray an inaccurate version of the past and are intimidating and insulting to large numbers of citizens makes a strong statement.

Perhaps no statue, memorial, or monument can tell a full and true story or represent everyone. Some people argue that we should not honor anyone with statues because all human beings are flawed and our views of them change over time. But Virginia's commission recommended replacing the Lee statue with one of another Virginian—a Virginian who made significant contributions through civic or military service. The commission encouraged individuals and groups all over the state to make suggestions. Nominations came in, and a panel narrowed the list to five finalists. What historic Virginian could best represent the people, values, and ideals of Virginia in 2020 and into the future?

The state's final choice was Barbara Rose Johns. Her likeness will stand in the US Capitol to remind visitors of what one person, even a very young person, can do. Barbara Johns's work isn't finished, and neither is America's.

EPILOGUE

Prince Edward County's story is one of determination and perseverance against centuries-old racism. It's a story of standing up for what's right, even when that means years of sacrifice. It's a story of what young people can do and the power they have to make a difference.

Prince Edward's story is also an example of how fragile our rights under the US Constitution are. It's an example of how a small group of Americans can work to deny another group of Americans their guaranteed right to equality under the law. Decades later, civil rights in the United States are still fragile and in danger. There are still millions of Americans who face discrimination every day. Some of that discrimination is intentional; some is unintentional. Some is built into our lives in ways that many people don't even see. It exists in business, in housing, in policing, in voting and elections, and in education. Over half a century after the Supreme Court's 1954 decision in *Brown v. Board of Education* and the cases that followed, most schools in the United States aren't truly integrated, and inequality in education is still with us.

There are no easy or quick solutions to these problems. But this doesn't mean that society cannot solve problems of inequality. A first step toward finding solutions is making more and more Americans aware that the problems are real—that while the court cases and civil rights laws of the 1950s and 1960s made great strides, they did not eliminate racism. People must be aware that there is work to be done. Individuals, older and younger, can help. We can all play a part in expanding awareness. Each of us can exercise our constitutional rights to make our voices heard just as Black students in Prince Edward County did years ago. Many young people today are doing just that.

Thousands of students across the country walked out of school in May 2018. They were protesting the widespread gun violence that had shattered families and changed the way children and their parents felt about kids going to school. The organizers were students at Florida's Marjorie Stoneham Douglas High School, where a gunman had killed seventeen people earlier that year. The students wanted action to stop a long series of school shootings in the United States. Parents and teachers joined the marches in some places. But everywhere, students took the lead. Many had studied the issue and could speak as well as any adult on what they thought should be done to stop mass shootings. They didn't have any immediate success in terms of new laws, but the leaders of the movement were determined to keep going. Their perseverance may make a difference over time, as perseverance did in Prince Edward County.

In 2020, young people in Philadelphia participated in demanding help for children locked out of education by the COVID-19 pandemic. The pandemic had pushed most schools to close their buildings and go virtual with little time to prepare. Virtual schooling made internet access for students critical. Children without internet or with slow internet found themselves in a situation similar to what Prince Edward County students had faced when their schools had closed. In 2020, children in families with access to computers and high-speed internet could move ahead in their education. Children in families without that technology quickly fell behind. Concerned teachers, parents, and students organized a march outside Comcast headquarters in Philadelphia. The enormous internet and cable company already had programs in place to provide low-cost internet to schoolchildren whose families could not afford high costs. But the young people and adults petitioned the very wealthy company to do more. It's difficult to measure the impact of a demonstration like that, but the television and newspaper reports on the march certainly made more Philadelphians aware of the need.

During the course of the year, Comcast increased its efforts to get schoolchildren online.[193]

Young people can make their voices heard without marching too. Many school districts today have one or more students on their school boards. Those representatives can speak for their fellow students, but only if those students let the representatives know about their concerns. Students can also attend school board meetings as some of the Moton strike leaders did. They can write letters or sign petitions and ask others to sign. So can their parents—the First Amendment to the US Constitution guarantees it.

Young people can and do make a difference on issues beyond education as well. They have spoken out on climate change, raised money to protect endangered animals, initiated programs to provide food and other necessities to people in need, and even taken risks to protect their fellow citizens.

In spring 2020, seventeen-year-old Darnella Frazier stood up for justice and a stranger's rights in Minneapolis, Minnesota. She and her young cousin happened upon a frightening scene as they walked to a convenience store. Police were holding a man on the pavement. He was "terrified, scared,"[194] Darnella said later. She sent her cousin into the store for safety and then pulled out her phone and started recording. She didn't know the Black man on the ground or the White police officer who held him there with a knee on his neck. She didn't know the other officers who stood watching. The Black man might have broken the law. He might not have. Either way, Frazier knew that what was happening on the street wasn't right.

Darnella Frazier was afraid as she recorded. She was afraid that the police would use their mace or pepper spray on her. She was afraid of violence. But for nearly ten minutes that must have felt like ten hours, she kept recording. Other people around her shouted at the police. Some took pictures. And then the man, George Floyd, stopped struggling. He was dead.

The police report said that officers had handcuffed Floyd after he'd resisted them and that they then had called an ambulance because he seemed to be having a medical problem. That might have been the end of the case no matter what witnesses said. But Frazier's recording told a much different story. It showed police ignoring Floyd's cries for help, ignoring bystanders' pleas for them to let the man breathe.

Like the Moton High School strikers in 1951 and 1969, Frazier had used her constitutional rights to confront government officials who violated the Constitution. She couldn't save George Floyd's life, but she could make the nation aware of his death. She posted her video on

Facebook, and news outlets everywhere showed parts of it over and over. (Frazier was awarded a 2021 Pulitzer Prize for "courageously recording the murder of George Floyd....")[195]

Millions of people were horrified and shocked. They couldn't imagine such a thing. After all, tens of thousands of police officers across the United States do their difficult jobs very well every day. But in some communities, no one was surprised by what they saw. They'd seen the same kind of thing before.

The news and Frazier's video spurred both people who were shocked and people who were not surprised to respond. Women and men of all ages, all backgrounds, and all racial identities—many of them very young—acted. They joined a new chapter of the civil rights movement that had begun in 2013. Known as "Black Lives Matter," the movement called for an end to White supremacy and encouraged local communities to step up to stop violence against Black people.

In June 2020, marchers gathered in cities and towns in the US and in other countries. Researchers reported later that well over 90 percent of those marches—many with hundreds of thousands of participants—remained peaceful.[196] These weren't extremists. They were ordinary people demanding change in policing, in race relations, and in the ways Americans look at the past and the symbols that represent it.

A Black Lives Matter protest in Washington, DC, 2020.

During the next year, many cities, counties, and states made reforms in police procedures. Whether those reforms will make a positive difference is not yet known. At the same time, civil rights leaders and ordinary Americans pushed for steps forward in other areas as well. Big steps and small.

Local and state governments have since dedicated time and money to look for intentional and unintentional racism in their policies, rules, and practices. Colleges and universities have done the same. So have many businesses. They are taking steps to make American ideals real. Local residents, students, and consumers—older and younger— are using their voices to encourage those changes. Those voices, even very young voices, can push all of us to learn more about the past and take steps toward a better future.

Thousands of people gather on Black Lives Matter Plaza in Washington, DC, 2020.

In Fairfax County, Virginia, fourth-grade students had an assignment surrounding the state's historic markers—iron signposts that commemorated important people, places, and events in state history. There were over 2,600 markers around the state. Fewer than 400 of them honored Black people, and none honored the young woman that the students had just learned about in class: Barbara Johns. That didn't seem right. "We felt that we should do something about it," one child said. When their teacher told them that the governor of Virginia was sponsoring a Black History Month Historical Marker Contest, they saw an opportunity and got busy. They made their voices heard by writing and signing petitions and asking others to sign. And they submitted dozens of designs for a Barbara Johns marker. Their interest, concern, and work paid off. They were among the winners of the contest.

A historic marker with information about Barbara Johns now stands outside the Robert Russa Moton Museum in Farmville, where Johns organized the 1951 strike. One

Black Lives Matter marches and demonstrations sprang up across the US in the summer of 2020. Well over 90 percent remained peaceful.

fourth grader said, "If people walk by, they're going to learn about her life and what she did to help America." The marker will have an impact going forward. It has already had an impact on the students who worked to have it placed there. "My voice was heard by very important people in the government," said another fourth-grade student. And another student said, "You never think that you can do something—but we did!"[197]

Barbara Johns believed in the power of young voices

as she told the Moton students in 1951 that they would be all right if they stuck together—the county jail wasn't big enough to hold them all. Francis Griffin and Sam Williams and hundreds of other young people in Prince Edward County believed in the power of young voices as they risked arrest and violence to demonstrate against injustice in 1963. Prince Edward's Black students showed their faith in the power of young voices when they went on strike in 1969 to once again demand better education. Memorials, statues, and markers can honor their courage and accomplishments and educate people about their history and ours. More importantly, each of us can continue their legacy by using our own voices to speak up for justice and equality today and going forward.

Acknowledgments

The Prince Edward County, Virginia, story was hidden in plain sight for decades. I taught American history in Virginia for years without knowing that civil rights heroes had waged a long and difficult battle for equality just a few hours' drive from my classroom. Fortunately, through the efforts of many remarkable men and women, that story is now being told. I hope that this book will be part of that telling. It would not have been possible without the generosity of people who gave of their time and expertise to assist me, and the courage of the survivors of the school struggle who have shared their experiences.

My thanks to Cainan Townsend at the Robert Russa Moton Museum in Farmville, Virginia, whose understanding of the events and knowledge of the region and its people were immensely helpful. Thanks also to Dr. J. Michael Utzinger at Hampden-Sydney College and Dr. Larissa Smith at Longwood University, who shared their time and expertise in reviewing my manuscript, and to Dr. Heather Lettner-Rust at Longwood for her help in locating images. I also appreciate my conversations with 1951 strike veteran Joan Johns Cobbs, who read the manuscript carefully and gave me a detailed review, and with Deloris Hendricks and James Ghee, survivors of the school closings. My thanks also to Dr. Melodie Toby, widow of Moses Scott, for her reading, and to Ken Woodley, former editor of the *Farmville Herald* and champion of the *Brown v. Board* Scholarship Program, for his enthusiasm and support. And I am very grateful to the many men and women who lived the Prince Edward experience, including Beverly and John Hines, and Phyllistine Ward Mosley, who have shared their stories and photos with me and with other researchers.

Thanks also to my agent, Susan Hawk, of Upstart Crow, and my editor, Kendra Levin, at Simon & Schuster, as well as the team of talented people who turn a manuscript into a real book. Special thanks to Katrina Groover for her patience with me, and to Hilary Zarycky for his interior design, art director Sarah Creech and illustrator Cannaday Chapman for bringing a beautiful cover into being, and Bara MacNeill for her keen eye and expertise in copyediting.

As always, I am grateful to my friends and family for their support and cheerleading, most especially my husband, Paul.

Time Line

1951

April 23 – Sixteen-year-old Barbara Johns leads a student strike at R. R. Moton High School in Prince Edward County, Virginia; students first demand a better school facility but then agree to sue the county for school desegregation with NAACP representation

May 21 – NAACP lawyers file a lawsuit in US District Court in Virginia—*Davis v. County School Board of Prince Edward County*

1952

February 25 – Oliver Hill and Spottswood Robinson argue on behalf of Prince Edward students in *Davis v. County School Board of Prince Edward County*, saying that the Virginia Constitution's requirement for segregation in education violates the US Constitution's Fourteenth Amendment

March 7 – US District Court rules in *Davis v. County School Board* that it finds "no hurt or harm" to either race, but orders the county to complete the promised new high school quickly; NAACP lawyers appeal to US Supreme Court

May 5 – US Supreme Court accepts the NAACP's appeal of the *Davis* decision; *Davis* is combined with four other school segregation cases known together as *Brown v. Board of Education of Topeka*

December 9 – NAACP lawyer Thurgood Marshall argues on behalf of plaintiffs in *Brown v. Board of Education* (including *Davis v. County School Board of Prince Edward County*)

1953

June 8 – US Supreme Court rules that an 1873 law banning segregation in Washington, DC, restaurants is still valid, and therefore barring Black customers from restaurants in the city is illegal

1954

May 14 – Martin Luther King, Jr., becomes pastor of the Dexter Avenue Baptist Church in Montgomery, Alabama

May 17 – US Supreme Court rules in *Brown v. Board of Education* (including *Davis v. County School Board of Prince Edward County*) that segregation based on race in public schools is unconstitutional

1955

May 31 – US Supreme Court rules in *Brown v. Board of Education of Topeka (2)* that school districts must move to desegregate "with all deliberate speed"

August 28 – Fourteen-year-old Emmett Till is murdered in Mississippi after accusations that he flirted with a White woman; the brutality of his murder gains national attention

December 1 – Rosa Parks is arrested after refusing to give up her seat to a White passenger on a Montgomery, Alabama, public bus; support for her stand results in a year-long boycott of the bus system by Black residents of Montgomery and national attention for Martin Luther King, Jr.

1956

May 3 – Prince Edward County Board of Supervisors declares that they will abandon public schools in order to preserve segregation

August 27 – Clinton High School in Tennessee becomes the first desegregated public school in a Southern state when twelve Black students enroll; several Black students leave school during the year because they and their families fear for their safety; after continued unrest, the school is destroyed by a bomb in October 1958

1957

January 10 – Sixty Black minsters and other leaders meet in Atlanta, Georgia, to organize nonviolent anti-discrimination, anti-segregation protests; they form the Southern Christian Leadership Conference with Martin Luther King, Jr., as president

March 25 – US District Court in Virginia grants Prince Edward County a delay in desegregating its schools

September 4 – Nine Black students (the "Little Rock Nine") try to enter Central High School in Little Rock, Arkansas, but are turned away by the Arkansas National Guard; President Eisenhower sends US Army troops to escort the students, who are harassed throughout the school year

September 9 – President Eisenhower signs the Civil Rights Act of 1957 to protect voting rights

1959

January 19 – Supreme Court of Virginia rules that the state constitution requires that there be public schools throughout the state and that the state cannot use public school funds to give tuition grants for private schools

May 5 – US Court of Appeals in Virginia orders the US District Court to require that Prince Edward County desegregate its schools beginning in September 1959

June 2 – Prince Edward County Board of Supervisors denies all funds for public schools

1960

February 1 – Four Black college students refuse to leave a Whites-only lunch counter in Greensboro, North Carolina; their action inspires other *sit-ins* there and in other states; over eighty students are arrested at sit-ins in Nashville and remain in jail rather than pay a fine

April 22 – US District Court rules that Prince Edward County may not give private school tuition vouchers to anyone while the county's public schools are closed

July 25 – Woolworth's lunch counter in Greensboro serves Black customers for the first time

November 14 – Six-year-old Ruby Bridges is the first Black student admitted to William Frantz Elementary School in New Orleans, Louisiana

December 5 –US Supreme Court rules in *Boynton v. Virginia* that segregation in bus terminals violates the Interstate Commerce Act

1961

May 4 – Black and White "Freedom Riders" begin traveling together to protest racial segregation on interstate buses; they face angry mobs in several Southern cities

1962

March 28 – Reverend Martin Luther King, Jr., visits Prince Edward County

September 10 – Supreme Court Justice Hugo Black orders

the University of Mississippi to admit Black student James Meredith; a violent riot erupts on the Ole Miss campus on September 30 when a White mob assaults US marshals protecting Meredith

1963

April – Protestors in Birmingham, Alabama, face tear gas, fire hoses, and police dogs in daily demonstrations

April 16 – After his arrest during protests, Martin Luther King, Jr., writes "Letter from Birmingham Jail," explaining and defending nonviolent civil action and calling on other clergy, including White clergy, for their support

June 11 – Alabama Governor George Wallace stands in a doorway to bar Black students from enrolling at the University of Alabama

June 12 – NAACP official and civil rights leader Medgar Evers is shot in front of his home in Jackson, Mississippi; he dies at a nearby hospital soon after

June – Attorney General Robert Kennedy hires William vanden Heuvel to negotiate and establish schools for all Prince Edward County children for the 1963–64 school year

July–August – Black students and adults demonstrate in Farmville

August 28 – Over 200,000 people gather on the National Mall in the March on Washington for Jobs and Freedom; Martin Luther King, Jr., delivers his "I Have a Dream" speech

September 15 – Terrorists bomb the 16th Street Baptist Church in Birmingham, Alabama; four young girls are killed and several other children are injured

September 16 – Prince Edward County Free Schools open

November 22 – President John F. Kennedy is assassinated in Dallas, Texas

December 2 – Virginia Supreme Court of Appeals rules in *Griffin v. County School Board of Prince Edward County* that the county has the authority to close its schools; NAACP lawyers appeal to the US Supreme Court

1964

March 30 – US Supreme Court hears arguments in *Griffin v. County School Board of Prince Edward County*

May 11 – Robert F. Kennedy visits Farmville, Virginia, and the Free Schools

May 25 – US Supreme Court rules in *Griffin v. County School Board of Prince Edward County* that the county schools must reopen in September

July 2 – President Lyndon Johnson signs the Civil Rights Act of 1964, banning discrimination in public places and in employment

September – Prince Edward County public schools reopen, desegregated but underfunded

December 10 – Martin Luther King, Jr., receives the Nobel Peace Prize

1965

February 21 – Civil rights and former leader in the Nation of Islam Malcolm X is assassinated in New York; his focus on Black identity and independence influences the Black Power movement after his death

March 7 – Police attack peaceful demonstrators on the Edmund Pettus Bridge as they march from Selma to Montgomery, Alabama, to protest voter suppression; scenes of the "Bloody Sunday" attack shock Americans; after negotiations and a court order, Martin Luther King, Jr., leads a successful march that reaches Montgomery on March 25

August 6 – President Lyndon Johnson signs the Voting Rights Act of 1965, ending literacy tests and allowing federal review of state and local voting laws and election practices

1967

August 30 – Thurgood Marshall, the NAACP attorney who argued the *Brown v. Board of Education* case before the Supreme Court, becomes the first Black justice of the US Supreme Court

1968

April 4 – Martin Luther King, Jr., is assassinated in Memphis, Tennessee; his murder sparks peaceful protests across the country and riots in over one hundred cities

April 11 – President Lyndon Johnson signs the Civil Rights Act of 1968, banning discrimination in housing

June 6 – Robert Kennedy is assassinated in Los Angeles, California, while campaigning for the Democratic presidential nomination

1969

April 23 – Students at R. R. Moton High School strike in support of a fired teacher and for more funding, better conditions, and Black representation on the county school board

Selected Bibliography

"10 Stories 50 Years Later." *Moton Magazine Project, Vol. 1,* 2014. https://drive.google.com/file/d/1IzyQHYc16pKStEOTUoxnqb_llg1ml4WK/view.

"All Eyes on Prince Edward County." *Moton Magazine Project, Vol. 3,* 2018. https://drive.google.com/file/d/1Sxo1M_DWcIq5Fo6uKcCsKaShgXvLBEOC/view.

Bonastia, Christopher. *Southern Stalemate: Five Years without Public Education in Prince Edward County, Virginia.* Chicago: University of Chicago Press, 2012.

Branch, Taylor. *Parting the Waters: America in the King Years 1954–63.* New York: Simon & Schuster, 1988.

Daugherity, Brian J., and Brian Grogan, eds. *A Little Child Shall Lead Them: A Documentary Account of the Struggle for School Desegregation in Prince Edward County, Virginia.* Charlottesville: University of Virginia Press, 2019.

Green, Kristen. *Something Must Be Done about Prince Edward County: A Family, a Virginia Town, a Civil Rights Battle.* New York: Harper Perennial, 2015.

Kanefield, Teri. *The Girl from the Tar Paper School: Barbara Rose Johns and the Advent of the Civil Rights Movement.* New York: Abrams Books for Young Readers, 2014.

"Learn." Robert Russa Moton Museum online. https:// motonmuseum.org/learn/.

Lee, Brian E. "A Matter of National Concern: The Kennedy Administration's Campaign to Restore Public Education to Prince Edward County, Virginia." PhD diss., University of North Carolina, 2015. https://libres .uncg.edu/ir/uncg/f/Lee_uncg_0154D_11805.pdf.

McCartney, Martha. "Africans, Virginia's First," In *Encyclopedia Virginia.* https://encyclopediavirginia.org /entries/africans-virginias-first/.

Minton, Bennett. "The Lies Our Textbooks Told My Generation of Virginians about Slavery." *Washington Post*, July 31, 2020. https://www.washingtonpost .com/outlook/slavery-history-virginia-textbook/2020 /07/31/d8571eda-d1f0-11ea-8c55-61e7fa5e82ab _story.html.

"Panel to Hear Ideas for Replacing Virginia's Lee Statue in US Capitol." *Associated Press*, November 13, 2020. https://www.nbcwashington.com/news/local/panel-to -hear-ideas-for-replacing-virginias-lee-statue-in-us -capitol/2471077/.

Pierce, John. "The Reasons for Secession: A Documentary Study." *American Battlefield Trust.* https://www .battlefields.org/learn/articles/reasons-secession.

Robert Russa Moton Museum. https://motonmuseum.org/.

Seidule, Ty. *Robert E. Lee and Me: A Southerner's Reckoning with the Myth of the Lost Cause.* New York: St. Martin's Press, 2020.

Serwer, Adam. "The Myth of the Kindly General Lee." *The Atlantic,* June 4, 2017. https://www.theatlantic .com/politics/archive/2017/06/the-myth-of-the-kindly -general-lee/529038/.

Smith, Bob. *They Closed Their Schools: Prince Edward County, Virginia, 1951–1964.* Chapel Hill: University of North Carolina Press, 1965.

Stokes, John A., Lois Wolfe, and Herman J. Viola. *Students on Strike: Jim Crow, Civil Rights, Brown, and Me.* Washington, DC: National Geographic, 2008.

Sullivan, Neil V. *Bound for Freedom: An Educator's Adventures in Prince Edward County, Virginia.* New York: Little, Brown and Company, 1965.

"Their Voices, Our History." *Moton Magazine Project,* Spring 2016.

Titus, Jill Ogline. *Brown's Battleground: Students, Segregationists, and the Struggle for Justice in Prince Edward County, Virginia.* Chapel Hill: University of North Carolina Press, 2011.

Townsend, Cainan. Author interview, February 9, 2021.

Vaughn, Wally G. *Negro Students Locked Out of Public Schools for Five Years, September 1959–September 1964: Prince Edward County, Virginia, Oral Accounts.* In Due Season, Inc., 2018.

Woodley, Ken. *The Road to Healing: A Civil Rights Reparations Story in Prince Edward County, Virginia.* Montgomery, AL: NewSouth Books, 2019.

Recommended Reading

For Everyone:
Visit the Robert Russa Moton Museum at https:// motonmuseum.org/

For Young Readers:
The Girl from the Tar Paper School: Barbara Rose Johns and the Advent of the Civil Rights Movement; Teri Kanefield

Students on Strike: Jim Crow, Civil Rights, Brown, and Me; John A. Stokes, Lois Wolfe, and Herman J. Viola

For Primary Sources:
Negro Students Locked Out of Public Schools for Five Years, September 1959–September 1964: Prince Edward County, Virginia, Oral Accounts; Wally G. Vaughn

A Little Child Shall Lead Them: A Documentary Account of the Struggle for School Desegregation in Prince Edward County, Virginia; Brian J. Daugherity and Brian Grogan, eds.

For a Detailed Account and Analysis:
Southern Stalemate: Five Years without Public Education in Prince Edward County, Virginia; Christopher Bonastia

Brown's Battleground: Students, Segregationists, and the Struggle for Justice in Prince Edward County, Virginia; Jill Ogline Titus

For the Steps Forward Since the 1990s:

The Road to Healing: A Civil Rights Reparations Story in Prince Edward County, Virginia; Ken Woodley

For Examples of Misinformation in School Texts:

Virginia: History, Government, Geography; Spotswood Hunnicutt Jones and Sidman P. Poole Francis Butler Simkins

Endnotes

Chapter 1

1 Smith, 28–30.
2 Titus, 3.
3 Green, 42.
4 Smith, 32.
5 Barbara Johns, "Recollections," in Daugherity and Grogan, 39, 45.
6 Ibid., 46.

Chapter 2

7 McCartney, "Africans, Virginia's First," in *Encyclopedia Virginia*, https://encyclopediavirginia.org/entries/africans -virginias-first/.
8 Seidule, 32.
9 Thompson, "The Reconstruction Era in Prince Edward County," *Farmville Herald*, September 3, 2004. http://www .fpehs.org/pewords.html#The%20Reconstruction%20Era %20in%20Prince%20Edward%20County.
10 Seidule, 66–67.

Chapter 3

11 Stokes, 29.
12 Ibid., 7–8.
13 Branch, 8–9.
14 Johns, "Recollections," in Daugherity and Grogan, 46.
15 Ibid.

16 Stokes, 41.

17 Ibid., 21.

18 Vitug, Eric, Ed. "Dorothy J. Vaughan." NASA, May 24, 2017. https://www.nasa.gov/langley/hall-of-honor/dorothy -j-vaughan.

19 Ibid., 63–70.

Chapter 4

20 Smith, 8–13.

21 Ibid., 53–54.

22 Ibid., 51.

23 Johns and Carrie Stokes, "Letter from the Moton High School Strike Leaders," in Daugherity and Grogan, 47.

24 Smith, 48.

25 Ibid., 39.

26 Smith, 60.

27 Smith, 51.

28 Ibid., 53.

29 Stokes, 98.

30 Ibid., 101–104.

31 "A Problem Becomes an Issue," *Farmville Herald*, May 8, 1951, in Daugherity and Grogan, 50.

32 Stokes, 107.

33 Smith, 70.

34 "Davis v. County School Board of Prince Edward County," in Daugherity and Grogan, 58.

Chapter 5

35 Harry Byrd, "Statement of Harry F. Byrd, May 17, 1954," in Daugherity and Grogan, 67.

36 "Supreme Court Decision," *Farmville Herald*, May 21, 1954, in Daugherity and Grogan, 69–70.

37 Bennett Minton, "The Lies Our Textbooks Told My Generation of Virginians about Slavery," *Washington Post*, July 31, 2020. https://www.washingtonpost.com/outlook/slavery-history-virginia-textbook/2020/07/31/d8571eda-d1f0-11ea-8c55-61e7fa5e82ab_story.html.

38 Pierce, John. The Reasons for Secession: A Documentary Study." *American Battlefield Trust*, https://www.battlefields.org/learn/articles/reasons-secession.

39 Bennett Minton, "The Lies Our Textbooks Told My Generation of Virginians about Slavery," *Washington Post*, July 31, 2020. https://www.washingtonpost.com/outlook/slavery-history-virginia-textbook/2020/07/31/d8571eda-d1f0-11ea-8c55-61e7fa5e82ab_story.html.

40 Woodley, 14.

41 James Allen interview in Vaughn, 447.

42 "Byrd Calls on South to Challenge Court," *New York Times*, February 26, 1956, in Daugherity and Grogan, 84.

43 Prince Edward County Board of Supervisors, "Declaration and Affirmation," May 3, 1956, in Daugherity and Grogan, 88.

44 Smith, 129–130, 183.

45 Green, 94–95.

46 Titus, 35.

47 "With Profound Regret" in Daugherity and Grogan, 112.

48 Green, 83–84.

Chapter 6

49 Warren (Ricky) Leroy Brown interview in Vaughn, 67.

50 Shirley Jackson Brown interview in Vaughn, 85–86.

51 Douglas Metteau Vaughan interview in Vaughn, 107–108.

52 Ibid., 109.

53 Green, 101.

54 Titus, 39.

55 Ibid., 48.

56 Ibid., 48–49.

57 Green, 104–107.

58 Ibid., 106–111.

59 Flossie Scott White Hudson interview in Vaughn, 197–198.

60 Mildred Womack Patterson interview in Vaughn, 366.

Chapter 7

61 Warren Brown interview in Vaughn, 67.

62 Shirley Jackson Brown interview in Vaughn, 86.

63 Vaughan interview in Vaughn, 108–109.

64 Jerry "Monster" Smith interview in Vaughn, 143.

65 Sylvia Oliver interview in Vaughn, 105.

66 Carrie Clark Bland interview in Vaughn, 97.

67 Katharin Troth. "Make Your Own Road," *Their Voices, Our History,* Spring 2016, 52.

68 Martha Carrington Morton interview in Vaughn, 373.

69 Dorothy Lockett Holcomb interview in Vaughn, 349–350; Green, 152.

70 Oliver interview in Vaughn, 105–106.

71 Charlotte Herndon Womack interview in Vaughn, 102.

72 Lillian Gloria Jordan Johnson interview in Vaughn, 279–280.

73 Jackson Brown interview in Vaughn, 87.

74 Angeles Wood Christian interview in Vaughn, 402–404.

75 Arnetta Coleman Winston West interview in Vaughn, 47–49.

76 Barbara Jamison Orr interview in Vaughn, 48–49.

Chapter 8

77 Lesley Griffin, "Letter to President Eisenhower and Response," August 20 and 29, 1959, in Daugherity and Grogan, 120.

78 "First County to Give Up All Its Public Schools," *U.S. News and World Report*, June 22, 1959, in Daugherity, 116.

79 Jean M. White, "Prince Edward Is Deadly Serious on Keeping Schools Closed." *Washington Post, Times Herald*, October 11, 1959, A12.

80 Sheila Shield, "High Hopes, Faith Help Fight Cancer," *Afro-American*, April 19, 1960. https://news.google.com /s?nid=2238&dat=19600419&id=vb8lAAAAIBAJ&sjid= yvQFAAAAIBAJ&pg=925,1450355.

81 Titus, 81.

82 Ibid., 86.

83 Smith, 255–256.

84 Arthur Lee Foster interview in Vaughn, 248–252.

85 Titus, 89–90.

86 Ibid., 67.

87 Ibid., 72–73, 78–80.

88 Ibid., 63.

89 Ibid., 39.

90 Ibid., 161.

Chapter 9

91 "1960 Democratic Platform," July 11, 1960. https://www
.presidency.ucsb.edu/documents/1960-democratic-party
-platform.

92 John Kennedy, October 1, 1960. https://www.presidency
.ucsb.edu/documents/question-and-answer-period
-following-remarks-senator-john-f-kennedy-bean-feed
-minneapolis.

93 Brian Lee, "A Matter of National Concern: The Kennedy
Administration's Campaign to Restore Public Education
to Prince Edward County, Virginia." PhD diss., University
of North Carolina, 2015, 62. https://libres.uncg.edu/ir
/uncg/f/Lee_uncg_0154D_11805.pdf.

94 John Kennedy, press conference, February 8, 1961. https://
www.jfklibrary.org/archives/other-resources/john-f
-kennedy-press-conferences/news-conference.

95 Robert Kennedy, "Law Day Address at the University
of Georgia Law School," May 6, 1961. https://www
.americanrhetoric.com/speeches/rfkgeorgialawschool
.htm.

96 Robert Kennedy, address at Kentucky's Centennial of the
Emancipation Proclamation, March 18, 1963. https://www
.justice.gov/sites/default/files/ag/legacy/2011/01/20/03
-18-1963Pro.pdf.

97 Green, 178.

98 Smith, 237.

99 Martin Luther King, Jr., "Virginia's Black Belt," April 14,
1962, in Daugherity and Grogan, 155, 153.

100 "The Closed Schools," in Daugherity and Grogan, 141.

101 Alfred Klausler, "The Shame and the Glory," in Daugherity and Grogan, 156–157.

102 Samuel Williams interview in Vaughn, 10–13.

103 Smith, 232.

104 Bonastia, 195.

105 Betty Jean Ward Berryman interview in Vaughn, 124.

106 Ibid., 124–126.

107 Brenda Smith Potter interview in Vaughn, 174.

108 Sullivan, 6.

Chapter 10

109 Bonastia, 142.

110 Ibid., 145.

111 Titus, 130.

112 Ibid., 139.

113 Sullivan, 1, 6–7, 15.

114 Ibid., 12.

115 Barnes, J. *Equality Under the Law: The Lost Generation of Prince Edward County.* Encyclopedia Britannica Films, 1965.

116 Ibid., 19.

117 R. O. Walker, letter to the editor, *Farmville Herald*, November 27, 1962, in Titus, 106.

118 Moss, "Address to the Charlottesville Chapter," October 25, 1962, in Daugherity and Grogan, 161.

119 Titus, 95–96.

120 Ibid., 106–107.

121 Ibid., 107–108.

122 Sullivan, 21–22.

123 Ibid., 2, 42, 49–50.

124 Ibid., 65.

125 Ibid., 45, 65.

126 Ibid., 78–79.

127 Ibid., 71–72.

128 Titus, 106.

129 Sullivan, 59.

130 Bonastia, 154.

Chapter 11

131 William vanden Heuvel, "The Prince Edward County Situation," March 1964, in Daugherity and Grogan, 186.

132 Anthony Farley interview in Vaughn, 145–146.

133 Ibid.

134 Travis Dawson Harris, Jr., interview in Vaughn, 221–224.

135 John Hurt interview in Vaughn, 544.

136 Bonastia, 157.

137 Sullivan, 109–110.

138 Bonastia, 152.

139 Ibid., 154.

140 Oreatha Wiley Banks interview in Vaughn, 157; Sullivan, 195.

141 Sullivan, 140–146.

142 Titus, 158.

143 L. Francis Griffin, "Letter to William vanden Heuvel," November 25, 1964, in Daugherity and Grogan, 208–209.

Chapter 12

144 Bonastia, 140.

145 Ibid., 165.

146 Peggy Bebie Thomson, "A Fresh Wind in Farmville," April 1964, in Daugherity and Grogan, 190.

147 Vanden Heuvel, "The Prince Edward County Situation," March 1964, in Daugherity and Grogan, 183.

148 Sullivan, 194.

149 Titus, 163–166; Bonastia, 227–228.

150 Griffin, "Letter to vanden Heuvel," November 25, 1964, in Daugherity and Grogan, 208–209.

151 Nancy Adams, "Speech at Annual Meeting of the American Friends Service Committee," October 30, 1965, in Daugherity and Grogan, 213–215.

152 Bonastia, 227.

153 Titus, 167.

154 Sullivan, 167.

155 Bonastia, 228.

156 Titus, 178.

157 Ibid., 167.

158 Bonastia, 235.

159 Ibid., 236.

160 Ibid., 236–237.

161 Ibid., 240.

162 Ibid., 239–240.

Chapter 13

163 Stokes, 119.

164 Hilton Howard Lee, Sr., interview in Vaughn, 501.

165 Dorothy Lee Allen interview in Vaughn, 504–505.

166 Green, 240–241.

167 mirshahids1, "Democrats Honor Farmville's First African American Attorney," *ABC 8 News*, March 1, 2018. https://www.wric.com/news/democrats-honor-farmvilles-1st-african-american-attorney/.

168 Bonastia, 248.

169 Woodley, 34.

170 Titus, 206.

171 Warren Brown interview in Vaughn, 70–71.

172 John Hurt interview in Vaughn, 545–546.

173 Bonastia, 261.

174 Harris interview in Vaughn, 225–226.

175 Dorothy Lee Allen interview in Vaughn, 504–506.

176 Titus, 221.

177 Angeles Wood Christian interview in Vaughn, 403–404.

178 Sylvia Oliver interview in Vaughn, 106–107.

179 Leslie F. "Skip" Griffin, Jr., LinkedIn profile. https://www
.linkedin.com/in/leslie-f-skip-griffin-jr-154a355a/.

180 Michelle Fan, "Black History Month: How the Kindness of Strangers Changed One Man's Life," Right at Home Blog, February 16, 2017. https://www.rightathome.net/blog/how-the-kindness-of-strangers-changed-a-life.

181 Jo Ann Randall interview in Vaughn, 93.

Chapter 14

182 Townsend interview, Titus, 210–211.

183 Katharin Troth. "Make Your Own Road," *Their Voices, Our History,* Spring 2016, 52.

184 Green, 10.

185 House Joint Resolution No. 613, February 13, 2003. https://www.doe.virginia.gov/administrators/superintendents_memos/2003/inf105a.pdf.

186 Woodley, 146.

187 Bonastia, 128.

188 Woodley, 147, 143.

189 House Joint Resolution No. 728, February 24, 2007. https://lis.virginia.gov/cgi-bin/legp604.exe?071+ful +HJ728ER.

190 Pamela Stallsmith, "The Rev. L. Francis Griffin," *Richmond Times-Dispatch*, February 1, 2000, updated September 19, 2019. https://richmond.com/the-rev-l-francis-griffin /article_301894d8-6b0f-11e2-b51f-001a4bcf6878.html.

191 Adam Serwer, "The Myth of the Kindly General Lee," *The Atlantic*, June 4, 2017. https://www.theatlantic.com /politics/archive/2017/06/the-myth-of-the-kindly -general-lee/529038/.

192 "Panel to Hear Ideas for Replacing Virginia's Lee Statue in US Capitol." *Associated Press*, November 13, 2020. https:// www.nbcwashington.com/news/local/panel-to-hear-ideas -for-replacing-virginias-lee-statue-in-us-capitol/2471077/.

Epilogue

193 Maddie Hanna. "Protesters Demand That Comcast Provide Internet Access to All Philly Kids." *Philadelphia Inquirer*, August 17, 2021.

194 Rachel Treisman. "Darnella Frazier, Teen Who Filmed Floyd's Murder, Praised for Making Verdict Possible." NPR, April 21, 2021. https://www.npr.org/sections/trial -over-killing-of-george-floyd/2021/04/21/989480867 /darnella-frazier-teen-who-filmed-floyds-murder-praised -for-making-verdict-possible.

195 "The 2021 Pulitzer Prize Winner in Special Citations

and Awards." The Pulitzer Prizes. https://www.pulitzer
.org/winners/darnella-frazier.

196 Sanya Mansoor. "93% of Black Lives Matter Protests Have
Been Peaceful, New Report Finds." *Time*, September 5,
2020. https://time.com/5886348/report-peaceful-protests/.

197 Hannah Natanson. "A Civil Rights Hero Lacked a
Historical Marker. Then a Class of Virginia Fourth-
Graders Spoke Up," *Washington Post*, February 24, 2021.
https://www.washingtonpost.com/local/education/barbara
-johns-historical-marker/2021/02/24/be0cf788-72b4
-11eb-b8a9-b9467510f0fe_story.html.

Index